Sungbook

A Collection of
Korean Stories

By

Suil Kang

Branden Books, Boston

Library of Congress Cataloging-in-Publication Data

Suil, Kang.
  [Essays Selections]
Sungbook : a Collection of Korean Stories / by Suil Kang.
  pages cm
ISBN 978-0-8283-2498-4 (pbk. : alk. paper) -- ISBN 978-0-
8283-2499-1 (e-book)
1. Korea--Social life and customs. I. Title.

PS3619.U388A6 2013
814'.6--dc23

    2013030107

Paperback ISBN 9780828324984
E-Book ISBN 9780828324991

Branden Book
PO Box 812094
Wellesley MA 02482
www.brandenbooks.com

2

Contents

A Playground

Kyonghee was the leader. She was the oldest, tallest, and strongest among a half dozen or so boys and girls who played together on the streets of their village in the outskirts of Seoul whenever they could get away from their chores and errands. They played *The Thirty-eighth Parallel*. A half of the group was to run from one end to the other end of a rectangle drawn on the ground, thereby unifying the Korean peninsula; the other half were soldiers stationed in narrow strips along the rectangle. Their duty was to kill, by stretching their limbs and touching, those who attempted to pass their stations. The trick for would-be unifiers was to occupy the soldiers' attention with close encounters with them, while other comrades successfully crossed the station, or cause the soldiers to lose their balance and breach the lines of their station. It would then become a "free station," free of the guards. The children also played toppling the stones. They lined up stones and then threw their stones from twenty feet or so, making sure their inching toes did not cross the line of demarcation drawn in the dirt. It required eye, hand, and body coordination; some were just natural at it. At dusk they played hide-and-seek: the base was the electrical pole where wires crisscrossed and moths ceaselessly dashed onto one dangling light bulb at its very top. Not far from it was the main crossroads of the village, where housewives sat on straw mats with their legs crossed under their long skirts and talked nonstop about all things that came to their purview, while trimming vegetables, or just resting after a long day.

By the summer of Kyonghee's fourth grade in 1970, the women at the crossroads made slight remarks that she was getting too old to be horsing around with her younger friends. Without much resistance, she gave up the games played on the

4

streets, for they were indeed not as much fun for her as they used to be. Instead, she began to lead her friends to the hills and valleys around their village; this was not a little child's game.

In mornings, Kyonghee attended a Bible school. A minister who recently moved to her village had opened it. Afterwards, she would lead her friends to the outskirts of their village, out of the women's view. Sometimes they flew down the hills, crossed the stream below, and explored the mountains on the opposite side of theirs. Sometimes they hiked up from their village to the southern ridges of the Bookak Mountains, where they came across the soldiers guarding the Blue House far below. At first, they watched the soldiers closely. They then gingerly approached them, making a game of who would first speak to them and elicit a response. When the soldiers grinned, grunted, or gave guttural responses, the children scurried away tickled.

On the days when Kyonghee did not lead her friends to the mountains, she sometimes could not resist intervening in the games of her younger friends and showing off her skills.

"See, this is how you do it," she said to Sunhee, the new queen of paper tiles after Kyonghee's abdication, who was losing her best tiles to Jeeyoung. Kyonghee thumped and flipped a tile, one of Jeeyoung's, which was flat on the ground; Sunhee nodded with admiration.

"It's not fair," Jeeyoung whimpered. It was made from a cardboard box, which her father brought home after her insistent and tireless cajoling. With it she had flipped many of Sunhee's and was about to become a new queen when she missed her last target and lost her turn and Kyonghee intervened. She basked in her glory.

"See, I told you. Hardness isn't everything. It has to be heavy, supple, and layered, like this one." She proudly showed

5

off her handsome tile, made from layers of newspaper strips. Balanced and worn, it had that dignified look of an old soldier. Kyonghee shifted to find another target. It was again one of Jeeyoung's.

"It's not fair." Jeeyoung protested louder. Indeed, in eyeing Jeeyoung's tile again, when there were also Ayoung's and Sunhee's, Kyonghee was not being fair. Besides it was an easy one, for it was on a pebble and thus had a little tilt. Anyone old enough to walk could have flipped it.

"Stop your grousing! She is just showing us how to do it," chimed Ayoung, an incurable commentator who aired every bit of intelligence, suppositions, and gossip that lit up in her brain. She always volunteered to summarize whatever was happening in their group. Kyonghee knit her eyebrows. She stood up and straightened herself.

"Here, it's your turn." She nudged Sunhee forward and placed the tiles back to where they were before she stepped in. Kyonghee was a leader, their General Yi Soonshin. Her friends followed her not only because she was the oldest, the tallest, and the strongest, but also because she was fair and had a generous mind.

Kyonghee had lived in her village on the hills of Sungbook ever since she could remember. She lived with her mother and three older sisters; her father lived with a new wife, whom, she had heard, he brought home shortly after she was born. She did not miss him, unlike her older sisters, who visited his sweater factory often. They proudly reported how generous he was and how his business was growing by leaps and bounds since he obtained an export license. But Kyonghee cared for neither their news nor him. She felt awkward when she saw him now and then in the company of her mother and sisters.

Late one afternoon on a hot August day, her mother called Kyonghee to her room.

"Try this on," Mrs. Ha said, holding up a new dress.

"Why? I don't want to." Kyonghee had been left to herself most of the time and was not required to act girlish. She could not remember the last time she wore a dress or a skirt.

"Can you just listen? Your father has a business trip coming up and wants to see you all, especially since it will be an overseas trip. We are to meet him tomorrow."

"I don't want to!"

The last time they met, he acted as if he loved her, caressing and hugging her. She did not like that. He was no father to her. He should not have acted that way. In her mind, she was fatherless. Seeing him once in a while did not change that. She had no memory of him and was not like her sisters, who resented their home on poor hills and stayed out of it as much as they could, studying in the libraries, window shopping, and visiting the factory, and their friends' home. But Kyonghee loved her village up in the mountains, close to the sky, and God.

"Shh, now, try it."

Mrs. Ha unzipped the dress and held it for her youngest daughter. Kyonghee stepped into it, thinking of her father. He now had two sons. Why couldn't he leave her alone? Why would he want to see her and pretend he cared for her?

The dress drooped on her although it was pretty, with pleats below the waist and a white round collar. But it just did not look right on her. She could tell her mother thought it too, for while she said it looked pretty on her, she kept tugging it this way and that until Kyonghee hollered at her to stop it.

The next morning, when Kyonghee returned from the Bible school, her mother told her to get ready. Her older sisters were already dressed and making sure they looked their best.

"I don't want to go."

"Get ready. I will buy you your favorite dish, I promise."

"I don't want to."

The last time Mrs. Ha made Kyonghee go, it was a disaster. Kyonghee moved glacially and whimpered every hundred yards or so. She barely greeted her father and then sat silently throughout the lunch. She did not even finish her favorite noodle dish, *chjachangmyun*. Kyonghee reflected badly on her, Mrs. Ha remembered. What if she stayed home? Her father did not know her as well as the other girls. Kyonghee was two when they moved out to Sungbook, after her husband announced he had a new wife and a newborn. But for the girls, she would not see him either, thought Mrs. Ha. The misery and humiliation he caused her were still fresh in her memory. But the girls needed his support, and she had difficulty enough in maintaining her household from what he gave her. She had to go, but did not need to bring Kyonghee with her.

"O.K., will your behave? Can you promise me?"

"Yes!"

Kyonghee bounced around to be helpful to her mother and sisters. She cheerily walked them out and stayed home turning away her friends who came looking for her with a promise for a long hike tomorrow. When her mother returned home, she handed Kyonghee a bag of her favorite cookies, crispy crackers lodged with seaweed bits, peanuts, and sesame seeds. She said that her father asked about her and that she was to go with them the next time, without fail.

8

The next day, Kyonghee led her friends - Sunhee, Ayoung, Jeeyoung, and Samyoung - farther into the Bookak Mountains than they had ever gone before. They meandered through innumerable shades of green leaves, sunlit translucent green to dark canopies beneath the shadows of other overlapping leaves. When the forest thinned, they ran into a handsome mosaic wall, made of hewn granite. Slender black tiles with lotus designs on their sides capped the top of the wall. It was the back of a large traditional house below. The wall was shorter than Kyonghee, because it was on the top of the hill. It grew taller as it continued down the hill, becoming very high by the time it reached the gate on a flat part of the hill. Ayoung passed her fingers over the wall nearest her.

"It would not crumble, not like yours," said Jeeyoung. Ayoung tossed an angry look at her. But it was true that the wall of her house crumbled every rainy season. She was mute, and this was a rare occasion, for Ayoung seemed to be born to argue. She usually stated what was right and what was improper, and volunteered whatever information she had soaked up from wherever and however, the radio, books, cartoons, and anyone in her village.

"Look!" Kyonghee pointed to something over the wall. Ayoung and Jeeyoung tiptoed; Samyoung jumped and clung over the wall. In the front yard, before a large traditional building, women in *hanbok*, with their hair in tight buns, were sprucing up the house. It was a strange sight to see them perform such tasks in colorful, traditional dresses. Only beautiful actresses and singers on glossy calendars or special holiday TV programs wore such dresses.

"This must be Bookchungkak," said Kyonghee.

"Yeah, I heard the aunties talking about it. That's where President Park and his men come. It's quiet now, but they have big parties at night. You could hear the *kayakeum* then," Ayoung said.

The sound of *kayakeum* echoing in a still night arose in the children's mind. The music would start slowly, almost fitfully, would turn rapid, and turn and turn. President Park and his powerful men would sit before a long table laden with hundreds of exquisite dishes. Milky rice wine would flow from the slender neck of a round, porcelain jar. Pleasing. Just like the old days in Chosun.

"What's Bookchungkak?" asked Samyoung, the youngest and the only boy in this excursion. He asked questions the girls dared not out of diffidence, politeness, or embarrassment.

"I told you. It's a party-house. President Park comes here after he is done with working," said Ayoung.

"I will be like him." Samyoung straightened his shoulders and flexed his small arms. Kyonghee gave him a mean look.

"You can't be a president," he said, for Kyonghee's gaze made him nervous.

"She could too!" exclaimed Ayoung. Ignoring her, Samyoung continued with his imitation martial art, chopping the air with the blades of his hands while balanced firmly on his bent legs.

"Who are those women?" asked Sunhee. She had been quietly gazing over the wall.

"They must be *gisaeng*, you know, like Hwang Jinee. You know, the beautiful, smart *gisaeng*. She recited poetry," said Ayoung.

"Maybe like your Aunt, Sunhee," said Samyoung. He was referring to the younger sister of Sunhee's mother, who visited her family in very fancy clothes.

"Be quiet. You don't know anything," said Ayoung. She did not want Sunhee to be embarrassed and was sure no one else did either, regardless of those whispers about her aunt in their village.

"Did you ever see her in *hanbok*? Did you ever see her in *hanbok*, Sunhee?" asked Ayoung.

"No," Sunhee answered quietly. She was almost always quiet.

"You never saw her with a *kayakeum* either, right?" asked Ayoung.

"That means nothing. She doesn't visit her house that often anyway," said Jeeyoung.

"Sure, but it says something," insisted Ayoung, while she was somewhat taken aback and watched Jeeyoung. Her father worked at the police station, and she often knew things about which Ayoung had no idea. Jeeyoung was making a little depression scratching the ground with the front of her right shoe. She was fidgety.

"Be quiet you all," Kyonghee yelled. She was grumpy. The house was deep in the forest for a reason. There was a reason why no one in their village discussed it in the open and only whispered about it in twos and three's; she had a reason why she never spoke of her father.

"Let's go!" Kyonghee led her friends away from the beautiful house towards a pond. They had found it in the beginning of the summer. The trickles from the pond formed several black puddles beneath it, and in them were innumerable tadpoles, which flitted across the unreflecting, black surface. Mesmerized, the children watched them.

In Minister Jang's Bible school, the children learned to recite the Lord's Prayer and sang joyously about the Jordan River. As she joined her friends in belting out hymns, Kyonghee wondered whether it was magical, different from the Han River. Why else

11

the clapping and joy about going there and crossing it? She must go there one day. It wouldn't do to ask the minister about it. The last time she asked a question, about how being reborn was different from coming out of a mother's belly, the whole congregation rocked in laughter and he had turned crimson red. It was during an evening service before the whole congregation, and she was responding to his invitation to ask questions when a few adults began to chuckle and little boys like Samyoung rolled with their hands on their bellies. Kyonghee did not know why her question was funny, but she was sorry to make the minister so embarrassed. She was to be careful about asking questions in church. As for the Jordan River, she would go there one day and see how it was different from the Han River.

When Kyonghee recited the Lord's Prayer from memory as Minister Jang taught his students to do, it made her feel calm and serene. She could not help but nod in agreement each time she came to the part about forgiving others as she hoped God would forgive her, although she could not think of anything straight off for which she needed anyone's forgiveness. She did not make all A's, but no one ever said you needed to ask forgiveness for not being the smartest. She could listen to her mother better, couldn't she? She should strive to. How about her father? There was the trouble. She did not like her father; she should ask for forgiveness. One day. Perhaps one day. Could she ever like him? Unlikely. One day? Unlikely.

Kyonghee opened her eyes after the Lord's Prayer, while others continued on with their personal prayers. What could they be asking so much from God? She could see, obliquely, Ayoung, Jeeyoung, and Sunhee too. They squeezed their eyes tight, as if His hearing depended on how tightly they closed them. She needed to not tug God's ear that way. The only thing she really wished for was for her family to be as it was before she was born. She had heard often how wonderful her father was then. It was impossible. Kyonghee closed her eyes and watched the incredibly changing shapes and colors that spiraled and streamed before her lightly closed eyes.

In addition to hymns and prayers, the children loved the minister's stories. Moses, Daniel, David, and Jonah, their stories were as fantastic, as entertaining as martial arts stories, like those about twin princesses somersaulting from rooftop to rooftop seeking revenge; an evil kung fu master who hurled icy cyclones from his palms; and the monkey king who could glide miles and miles riding a cloud, but who could not escape Buddha's palm.

Of the many biblical heroes, John the Baptist was their favorite. He was poor. He was free. He was like them, yet he was a prophet. He lived in the wilderness, wearing hides and eating locusts, and people thronged to see him. He was humble, humble as they were, or as they were constantly told to be. When people milled about him in awe, he said he was unworthy, not worthy to touch even the shoelaces of Jesus. Brave too, he died, rather than bow before an unjust king.

Kyonghee decided that they should pay homage to their hero before the summer ended. On the morning of August 15, while their mothers were busy with their morning chores and when the radio would soon carry President Park's commemoration of the patriots who died fighting for their country, the children grouped with their knapsacks at the western edge of their village. They flew down the steep path beyond the house of Mr. Kim, whose wife was sick and whose daughter stayed mostly inside. Crossing the narrow neck of the stream, far north of the large pool where the cool mountain water gathered before it thundered over massive cliffs spraying mist and foam, they climbed the uninhabited parts of the Mountains.

13

The modernity President Park urged onto his people at all costs began appearing on this side of the mountains. Men from their village and villages like theirs blasted the granite beneath the trees for a tunnel; it would connect this part of Seoul to a road behind the Blue House. A brand new road already encircled the hills, on top of which was a Buddhist temple. Abandoned, angular boulders in the fields next to the road were mute witnesses to Korea's push toward modernity.

Happy to be alone by themselves on the new road, which was closed to cars, the children walked in the middle of it. They soon wilted under the intense heat arising from the asphalt, like the gingkoes along the road that were recently planted. Kyonghee directed her friends towards the inner parts of the mountains behind the temple. She felt sorry for the little sticks of gingko. They could not up and move, unlike her.

In the valley below the temple, the children came upon what they were looking for: a swarm of grasshoppers. Some leaped and buzzed. Some on the tips of the grass swayed as one with the blades. Kyonghee punched little holes in the lids of the empty jars the children brought with them.

The initial catches were easy. The children dropped the grasshoppers that tickled in their closed palms into the jars. The peace of the valley was broken. The grasshoppers bounded helter-skelter and buzzed up like helicopters, but did not glide like the birds and did not fly far away. They landed on spots not distant from where they hopped.

The children spread and pursued them like disciplined soldiers. They did not miss many. Kyonghee, who had felt sorry for the wilting ginkgoes only a short while ago, had set apart the grasshoppers from all other things. When it became difficult to catch them, because even the laziest forsook the pest-infested

14

area, the children considered the result of their work. They had filled their jars. They had more than enough.

They began looking for a cleared spot and moved towards a bald ground near the road north of the temple. On their way, Ayoung suggested that the acorns on their path would make excellent appetizers. Recalling that all nuts they had tasted were delicious, especially when grilled, they agreed with eagerness.

Kyonghee built a fireplace, imitating her elders who built outdoor grills in summertime: she placed two large stones in parallel and the third at the end of them. Sunhee and Jeeyoung endeavored to crack open the acorns. Ayoung, Samyoung, and Sungwoon, Sunhee's little brother who often tagged along after her, scouted for twigs.

The acorns were hard to open. Small, they were difficult to hit; round, they rolled from the stone surface where they were placed. The children retrieved a few nuts after everything else was done: after the twigs were duly placed in the fireplace, and a thin grill was set across the stones. Even to the end, the acorns were miserly. Like a compact, old woman, they knew how to spoil their conquerors' expectations. The nuts showed no sign of softening. When they finally gave faint smoke, weary of the wait, Kyonghee salted them and took them off the grill. Sunhee and Samyoung were the first to taste. They spat them out.

"What's wrong?" asked Ayoung, and unable to wait the time it took for them to wipe their tongues, or to resist the temptation to know it herself, she dropped one into her mouth.

"Phut!" she spat it out.

Kyonghee bit into one. It was hard as the sand and bitter, and had none of that sweet nuttiness of walnuts, special treats on a winter holiday, or her favorite, grilled chestnuts, the taste of which she recalled when she gathered them. She rinsed her mouth. The others followed.

15

"The skin was the worst!" Ayoung volunteered as usual to summarize their experience. Off to one side, Samyoung, Sungwoon, and Jeeyoung began hurling the nuts and invented a game of who would throw them the farthest. Kyonghee soon got their attention when she grilled the grasshoppers.

Despite the ugliness of the crushed black mass in their jars and the fact that they had never heard of anyone eating locusts until Minister Jang's story, the children were full of expectations. The acorns were disastrous, but no one told them a story of eating grilled acorns. The grasshoppers were different. They heard the story of John the Baptist in the tent church, and in their mesmerized minds, the grasshoppers grew as a true delicacy, something rarely eaten but sworn by the initiates as an exalting experience. They did not know whether a Messiah was coming or going; they lacked, too, the courage to defy a king. But they could emulate the hero; they could eat the locusts in the wildness.

The grasshoppers burned quickly. Kyonghee moved them towards the edges of the grill, made sure their soft bellies were well cooked, and salted them. They looked far from appetizing. Charred, their black beady eyes looked enormous in their squat trunks - their spindly legs and airy wings had disintegrated. Kyonghee distributed the delicacy. Ayoung, Sunhee, and Jeeyoung, each gazed at her palm with revulsion.

"You girls are chickens," said Samyoung the boldest. He popped one into his mouth. Sungwoon quickly followed him. Sunhee, his older sister, gave him a look of exasperation, but he romped with pride after Samyoung.

"How is it?" asked Ayoung. The boys giggled.

"Try it," Kyonghee said and dropped one into her mouth. Ayoung and Jeeyoung followed, closing their eyes tightly as when they prayed. Sunhee demurred.

16

The grasshoppers tasted as they looked, and nothing like what they had imagined. Howsoever they desired to imitate their hero, whose image was deeply engraved in their minds, and however fervently they wished their play to be successful, the children did not go on pretending it was fun. No one wanted a second.

Kyonghee and her friends put out the fire stomping to make sure they left no trace of a flicker. They knew of the sorry state of Korea's mountains and had repeatedly heard the dangers of wildfires. Patriots, they would not further ruin their country. You saw two lands, they had heard, when you flew over from the Pacific. The first was green; it was Japan with its healthy mountains. The second, brown, was Korea with its mountains ravaged by the communists and the ignorant poor. The children knew better than to cause further damage to the mountains of their beloved country.

Moving away from her friends, Kyonghee walked in a field of grass and cast away the grasshoppers. Moses and Daniel and even small David, however much she and her friends cheered them on, their feats were beyond the ordinary. John the Baptist had seemed approachable. Kyonghee's mind, which had separated the grasshoppers from all other creatures, now let her see the killings she and her friends committed. In their feverish desire to imitate their hero in the wilderness, they turned buzzing gossamers of translucent green to ugly death.

Kyonghee led her friends away from the site of their grill. All of them were subdued: they had worked the whole morning, hoping to experience new delicacies. Even Ayoung was quiet, restrained by hunger and shame; yet she was hopeful, for Kyonghee had the foresight to direct each of them to bring different food items, pocketfuls of rice, spoonfuls of red pepper paste, and a few vegetables, and a tin pot for making the rice.

17

The children were preparing a new fireplace on a hill above the Buddhist temple, when Ayoung remembered the vegetable garden behind the temple: a little bit from it would absolutely enhance their picnic.

"We would play the monks, you know," she said. "We would take very little, not even noticeable."

Each of the children imagined their own versions of the enhancement to their meal and looked to Kyonghee. Green peppers and sesame leaves would indeed make great additions, she thought. Was it stealing? It didn't seem stealing, if they took only very little, not enough to be missed. They all could narrate endless stories about the monks who walked from one end of the Peninsula to the other end, surviving on the bounties of land. You had to be crazy to say the monks were thieves. Unlike Minister Jang's, these stories were in their blood. Their new play was guaranteed to succeed.

The children gingerly approached the garden. They were picking a few sesame leaves at the edge of it, when a young monk, a little taller than Kyonghee started toward them, with his fist in the air. He cursed at the top of his lungs.

"Animals! Bastards! . . . Fatherless bastards!"

He screeched and screamed, darting toward them. In his urge to catch them, he could not pause to wear properly his rubber shoes, *gomushin*, and they flapped against his heels. Stunned, the children watched him. He cursed better than anyone they had seen. The front halves of his untied gray surplice swung wildly beneath his heated round head. His fist, raised above his stubbly head, charged far ahead of the rest of him. Wonderstruck, they watched. They then bolted.

Kyonghee directed her friends and measured the water for the rice, while her mind kept circling round the monk. Buddha was compassionate. Limitlessly compassionate. He would not begrudge bits of vegetables from his garden. He would willingly share his. He would reason and show their wrong; he would not further embarrass those who were already ashamed. Where was the monk's compassion, his generosity? What did "fatherless" mean? It somehow made his curses sound a lot worse than they would otherwise be. Kyonghee thought and thought about his curses, while she quietly went on with the task of making the rice on an open fire. Sensing her mood, her friends were subdued. None of them had ever been so roundly cursed.

"That monk needs a good beating," said Samyoung, finally breaking their silence.

"He needs years of meditation," Ayoung added. Samyoung's remark had relieved her tension. She felt instinctively that words would help them. Kyonghee continued her silence. Silence regained.

"Fatherless bastard! That was a good one," said Samyoung, again breaking the silence and voicing words no one dared to repeat.

"Don't you ever say that!" Kyonghee snarled.

Her friends turned towards her. What was wrong with her?

"Do you know what it means?" she said, softening her tone to their looks of wonder. They shook their heads.

"It means, you are so unruly, even the sky cannot limit your evil," she said. "It means someone like me would never amount to anything!"

Seeing her agitation, her friends became greatly concerned and even more confused. They had never seen her father; that was true. That did not make her fatherless, did it? She must have a father, who did not have a father?

"Your mother must know your father," Samyoung said.

"Of course she knows her father, dummy," Jeeyoung said.

"You have seen him?" he asked.

"No, it's just that," she stammered.

"Be quiet, you two," Ayoung shouted, noting Kyonghee eyeing Jeeyoung with one of her meanest looks.

"That monk must be a yokel from the boondocks. He needs years of meditation," Ayoung added. She then moved towards Sunhee, who had begun to place stones on the corners of a large mat they had. Others followed their example and busied themselves with similar preparations for their meal.

Sunhee was the sensible one, although she never said much, thought Kyonghee. On the other hand, Jeeyoung had that particular way of getting under her skin, saying things out of the blue, things she must have heard from the adults who gathered around her father. Kyonghee then remembered her mother and sisters and the women of the village. They must be thinking the same thing as the monk! That she acted like someone who was fatherless.

She did not have a father. Simple. She did not care for one. That did not mean she should be cursed as fatherless. If she acted correctly, people would not think so, if she stopped running about the mountains with her friends. She would do her part. No one, not the monk, not the women in her village, not her mother and sisters, and not her own father would look at her and think "fatherless".

When the rice began to boil, Kyonghee tried to temper the flame and simmer it. She could not control the flame and extinguished it rather than risk burning the rice. It came out runny and unevenly cooked. Nevertheless, her friends savored their spoonfuls of rice garnished with a tiny dollop of hot pepper paste and bits of vegetables. They were eager to relieve their hunger and proud to eat in the field like adults after hard work. But they ate in silence, listening with all their senses to Kyonghee's silence.

They understood: their adventures had come to an end. They had their first and last meal in the mountains of Sungbook.

Kyonghee, young and full of optimism, strove to disprove the monk's blasphemy. She began to wear dresses and skirts. She stopped playing with her younger friends, who roamed the streets and hills about their village. She accompanied her mother without protest when her father requested her presence before him.

Minister Jang

Minister Jang climbed the hills in Sungbook on a sunny afternoon when the sky, trees, and even dirt looked bright and happy. A tattered brown leather briefcase bulged with hymnbooks, newsletters, and sermons in his right hand; a large Bible bound in black leather slanted backward under his left armpit. He was tall and broad shouldered, although the modesty of his occupation and prevailing custom of the time hid his large frame beneath his black suit.

Minister Jang had come to his new village about a month ago and set up a tent church on a flattened top of the highest hill on the west side of it. From one end of the cliff, he could see the whole of his new village: small houses, interspersed with small plots of vegetable gardens here and there, kept sloping downward like plates on a turtle's top, unless precipices which lined the stream far below thwarted their march. The wide stream below separated the hills on the side of this village from those on the opposite side, which were still lush and free from human encroachment. A thin metal sheet patterned with circular holes bridged the foothills leading to the village to the one lane, dirt road. It was the quickest way to reach the rest of Seoul, although a number of well, and less, trodden paths meandered through the hills around the village and eventually led to downtown Seoul, passing through other villages nestled in the Bookak Mountains.

Grandmother Lee was the Minister's landlady. She was one of a handful of residents who had lived in the village as long as anyone could remember. She knew every nook and cranny of the village and was one of the few whose favorite pastime was to find out everything about any new inhabitants of the village. She also had the knack of fanning every real and imagined story that passed through it, repeating and propelling it forward refurbished, in an eager, high-pitched voice to anyone near her. There was some consensus among her neighbors that her chatter had become worse, since her only son, Ducksoo, went down to Ulsan about two suns ago: it lacked a modicum of order, not that it ever was a well conceived discourse. Thus, when they ran into her on the street or when she joined the women at the crossroads, they fidgeted and cudgeled their brain to find an excuse to depart from her, an old lady who must be rather lonely, without palpable disrespect.

In grave and solemn Minister Jang, despite his habitual endeavor to be charitable and slow in anger, her unfounded excitement and volubility ran deeply against his grain. However, suppressing his first impression to flee from her, he rented two rooms from her, because he was a Christian, a minister at that, and because the rooms were separated from her quarters with a wood panel and had a different gate from hers. He and his family could come and go without running into her often; besides, it had city water, a luxury in a village such as this. His wife, a minister's wife, would not have to haul the laundry to the stream below like other women.

The gate to his home was ajar, and Minister Jang pushed it slowly and opened it further. His wife was doing laundry by the washstand, which was in the middle of the dirt yard. Naked bronze pipes, bestowed with glistening beads of water, beamed golden under the bright sunlight, and their newborn lay on a quilt under the lengthening shade of the house. Mrs. Jang, whose back was toward the gate, rose little by little from her squatted position, as she swished a pair of long trousers in a basinful of water and wrung it a small section at a time along the length. Swollen water drops pregnant with sunlight hung precariously

23

from the edges of a russet washbasin and the low concrete walls of the washstand.

His wife was tall and ungainly. A cotton strip was tied around her lengthy waist to keep her long skirt from getting wet; loose strands of hair licked her long face. Her small forehead and high cheeks glistened with sweat and water.

"Not tidy," thought Minister Jang. An image of a beautiful, serene woman rose in his mind. He had never seen such a woman, but images of famous beauties he had heard of and bits of recent beauties in *hanbok* on glossy papers of calendars had created indelible impressions in him, often leading him to make unfair comparisons with those about him.

The minister checked himself. His wife was a good, hardworking woman. She busied herself with chores, without complaining or seeking his attention. As he shut the gate, his wife patted her hair and unrolled her sleeves.

"Did you have a good trip?" she greeted, bowing slightly.

"Hhm."

"Lunch is ready. I'll bring it in a minute. Please do rest some," she said.

Mrs. Jang hurriedly tidied the laundry and the washstand; she would come back to it later. Her husband, stepping toward the baby, gestured to her to slow down and take her time. He gently raised the boy against his bosom. This wife was better than Sinyoung at least in this respect. For all of her beauty and pride, Sinyoung, the mother of his two daughters, failed to give him a son. Of course, he knew it was not the woman's fault when she did not produce a son. But as it has been so said for thousands of years, he was not to be blamed if he now and then slipped into this way of thinking. He was far better than most, for he would not say so in public.

Minister Jang closed his eyes and calmed the embarrassment that began to churn his mind. He should not have thought of Sinyoung; he should not have disturbed the memory of someone deceased. It was enough that he was remaking his life. Minister Jang refocused his gaze on the newborn, who was soundly asleep, not yet used to this side of life. The minister's own features, a broad forehead, strong cheeks, and wide, downwardly curving lips, were reflected back toward him. Uncharted, his son had infinite, or nearly infinite, possibilities. He needed to be strong for this son, thought Minster Jang. He was only forty-three. He had many years left. He could certainly rebuild his church and his family, and guide his son.

Mrs. Jang carried in lunch on a black lacquer table: a bowl of rice and dishes of fried tofu, fish cake, and spring kimchi. After a brief grace, Minister Jang ate silently. He preferred strong stews and hoped his wife would make them more often, but he rarely commented on food. Discourses on such things as food, clothes, and style were nonsense, and marks of silly people, who had nothing better in their head than the desire to show off, the likes of Sinyoung. After a few spoonfuls, he noticed his wife sitting next to the sliding doors, which led to the kitchen outside.

"Why don't you have some too?" he asked.

"Yes, I already had some," Mrs. Jang answered, echoing one of her usual replies. In fact, she ate at the table only during dinnertime, taking bits of side dishes her other family members would not take.

At about four o'clock in the afternoon when the brilliance of the day was almost spent, Youngmie and Jungmie came from school. Youngmie was tall and broad shouldered like her father and had Sinyoung's oval face. She was naturally graceful and carried herself with dignity. At eleven, she knew to say only "yeses" to her father, even though her eyes burned with hate

25

when his face was turned away from her. She layered one note after another, each memorializing his injustice and her humiliation. Jungmie, two years younger than her, looked much younger than her age and ethereal in her slender frame and perfectly crescent eyes. Her older sister was fiercely protective of her and acted as if she were her absent mother. The two sisters, their hair neatly braided in two strands and dressed smartly in sky-blue blouses and dark blue skirts, looked out of place in their new home, a makeshift structure with jutting panels and tar sheets.

Youngmie viewed her stepmother with a long, slow gaze. She was pinning a pair of trousers on a sagging clothesline after shaking them vigorously to further rid of water and wrinkles from them. As she stretched her arms and torso to properly hang them, she looked even longer than usual. At least it was not her mother who washed, cleaned, and cooked endlessly in this ugly house, thought Youngmie. Her father's black shoes were placed neatly on one side of the steppingstone.

"We are back from school, Mother," Youngmie greeted loudly and Jungmie followed in tow.

"Aiiie, is it so late, already?" said Mrs. Jang. "First go in and greet your father. I'll be done in a minute."

Leaning her shoulders backward, Mrs. Jang massaged her lower back. Another evening was approaching. She mentally went over the chores she had to do before nightfall. She had been with her new family for sixteen months. When the marriage proposal came in, she was confident she could fulfill the mother's role for the beautiful girls of the minister, an educated gentleman. As time passed, however, the distance between the girls and her seemed only to increase. Inexperienced and awkward, Mrs. Jang waxed and waned in her motherly role, at times acting unduly indulgent and friendly, and thus undermining her authority, and at other times, maintaining the distance they insisted between them. At such times, she had told herself that their resistance was only natural and she was to be patient. However, following the birth of her boy, Kwonil, she feared that they actually had reasons for resenting her. She had not known how it would be; she never suspected that her love for her boy would be so far beyond how she had striven to be a good mother for the girls. She also knew that her husband watched her closely and noted her progress with them. She closed her eyes and prayed. Briefly.

Minister Jang's tent church was about twenty by thirty feet large. On balmy spring days, its front and back flaps were folded up so that the breeze wafting down from the mountains would sweep through it. On hot days, the roof panels were opened up to further ventilate the church. A good number of trees - acacias, oaks, birches, alders, and others - were still near the church, making it the coolest part of the village.

After he set up the church, Minister Jang had visited each household in his new village, introducing himself and his church, and seeking the goodwill of his new neighbors. Downright hostile, a few of them hardened their postures as he approached them and sat stone-like as he greeted and requested them to come and try his church. They muttered, low but loud enough for him to hear, only when he turned to take his leave.

"A Jesus-nut! Don't we have gods of our own? Why, the old ones haven't worn out now, have they?"

"Church! Up here? Mus'be some minister to come all the way up here, hee hee, hee . . ."

Most of his new neighbors, however, were friendly and came to his church as he predicted. They were folks who instinctively obliged people above their station in life, unless some practical concern overrode their instinct to please. They strove to avoid even an appearance of conflict unless they were driven to a cor-

27

ner. Minister Jang did not ask anything from them but their presence. They willingly obliged him.

Each morning before sunrise, Minister Jang walked to church and prayed alone. Before the whitening light of the day dispelled the lingering obscurity of the night and outlined familiar trees, houses, and mountains and as the scent of misty dirt in the wind that swept through the church whistling and scattering spirits of the night bathed his senses, he sought the presence and guidance of God. These early hours were precious; they encouraged and nourished him.

A handful of adults and their children who got up early enough to follow their parents attended morning services. On Sundays, a few from his old church near the second rotary down the hills, past the largest open-air market in the district, came to his church. These old parishioners told him he was not abandoned. They reflected his belief that God did not forsake him. When the truth prevails, as it must, he would regain and reap beyond what he had lost. The old parishioners were also reminders of his life with Sinyoung, and his fall. He was lucky in a way, and he was grateful that it occurred after his parents' deaths, sparing them from witnessing, or sparing him the shame of witnessing them witnessing it and the renewed struggles on these hills of Sungbook.

When the sweetness of the acacias thickened the air, the children of the village enlivened Minister Jang's church. Freed from school, and open and eager to learn all new activities, they became his most ardent disciples. They knew to look toward the goodness he was pointing, without much ado about the messenger's serious and often heavy-handed demeanor. They cajoled their parents to attend the church and dragged their bemused mothers to church after helping them with dishes and tidying up the kitchen after their evening meals.

28

The adults came, pleased to witness their eager children and glad to be able to indulge their childish excitement. Besides, the minister's activities did not harm them. Rather, they tended to increase and create in them neighborly feelings for other human beings as they heard stories they already knew in their heart. And, although they heard them for the first time, they had known all along the stories of God, man, and spirit, now presented to them in western attire and with strange names and localities: that there were things beyond what the eyes of man could see. Before they heard of omniscient, omnipresent God, or meek Jesus, the belief that truth and goodness shall triumph in the end had sustained and nourished them. Poverty and wealth, pride and humility, death and resurrection, they dared not articulate, for they recoiled from the directness of their own speech as a finger recoils from a flame. But they had known them and cleaved to Minister Jang's strong and beautiful cadence. It swept them and caressed them with the promise that they were the children of God. He knew their true worth, and heaven was theirs. And reaping energy from his eager listeners, Minister Jang's cadence echoed and re-echoed in his own heart.

Minister Jang saw a group of women enthralled by a story being told by his landlady as he climbed the hills toward the crossroads of the village on a late afternoon in early August. Grandma Lee buzzed excitedly, underscoring special points with her fingers and forearms. He was right in his first impression about her. Of course her son fled, not caring enough about her to take care of her. Bustling about like an old buzzard in the middle of the road, she had no shame. He could tell, from the close formation of the women about her and from their expressions, she was relating something scandalous. Shame on her! Doing nothing other than gossiping in broad daylight and inciting unholy feelings. He passed them, greeting with a slight nod.

His wife was washing dishes by the washstand. Her long face seemed longer than usual and her greetings were inaudible. His son lay on a straw mat near the main room. The girls were looking out at nothing in particular, sitting at the edge of the wooden floor that connected their two family rooms. Entering his room, the Minister placed his Bible on the desk and his brief-case in a corner against it. When he came out, after he removed his jacket and socks, his wife had a basinful of cool water ready for him. It was refreshing to wash sweat and salt off his face and neck, and luxurious even to soak his tired, swollen feet in the water.

As he dried his feet and put on his slippers, Minister Jang asked if any thing had happened. His wife hesitated to answer this, one of his usual questions, as if she did not know how she should respond, but Youngmie, who had begun to braid Jung-mie's hair, interjected nonchalantly.

"Father, Grandma Lee was talking about us. Jungmie and I heard her. She said our mother ran away. I said it wasn't true! She said she knew all about it."

"Shh . . . quiet, Youngmie," said his wife. "Of course, she does not know," she added as she looked to him for guidance.

She was right in signaling him to hush the girls and to dis-cuss it later without them. It would be the prudent course, but the obstinacy that gripped him when a challenge or a threat was thrown before him spurred him on. He lacked the patience to wait until the excitement of the moment softened and said in his mind that the girls already knew whatever the unpleasant news was: they were inevitably part of it.

"It's okay, Youngmie, continue what you were saying," he said.

"She said, the old church, if the people at your old church didn't think you were good enough for them, you shouldn't be . . ."

"Youngmie, enough, please?" his wife pleaded. Youngmie ignored her.

"All of them were nodding their heads, Father!" said Youngmie, without looking to anyone particular.

"Father, will we move again?" Jungmie asked.

"Of course not! We'll be fine, Jungmie. Isn't that right, husband?" His wife said, looking to him, pleading for his assurance.

Anger shot up in him. Stupid, stupid women! Malicious and stupid. And his wife, timid, always timid, knew only to tremble before any and all disruption. What was he doing here? In anger he paced the front yard. He then turned towards the back, seeking his own space. Brambles and wild raspberries thrived there, a foothill against which the house was built. Bright red berries, late berries, floated amid a jumble of wiry branches. A few were separating, the calyx barely holding together crimson droplets. They looked about to burst. Lucky, lucky they would be, if before the looming fall they were plucked and dropped on far, far-away, fertile soil.

He should not fault his wife. She was only a simple woman hoping for peace, peace against the daunting odds, to which she was blind. What was the alternative? She was right, regardless of how she stumbled upon the solution in her habitual reaction to avoid conflict. Youngmie was different. She was like her mother, nonchalant, inviting and relishing in a dare. Quick to accuse, she had been accusing him, and he had known it. No, he should not malign a child. Rumors would have reached wherever he was. He would, must endure. Only with deeds far beyond reproach, he could respond. He was holy in Christ.

When Minister Jang returned to his family, he said he was sorry for his failures and shortcomings. All was his fault, he said, and God would protect them if they sought and believed in Christ. He asked his family to be with him and remember Christ in their renewed trial. Dignity and silence and love of Christ would protect them. That night, Minister Jang sang resoundingly with his family the songs about the Jordan River and Calvary. Their strong voices comforted the tired spirits of passersby, who were returning home late.

In the days that followed, fervent rumors whizzed in the village and made the hot August even more unbearable. Sinyoung was a beautiful woman who was turned out for adultery. No, it was a sad case of unbridled jealousy. The Minister drove her out in his passionate love and hatred. No, it was the wife who was unreasonable. He, being such a dedicated minister and old fashioned, did not know how to humor her. He had not the feeblest notion of his young wife's desires. A week or so later, a consensus emerged. The wife was too young and more beautiful than anyone like Minister Jang deserved. It was a shame, some people said, to be born so beautiful and poor and hoodwinked into marrying an old bore, and then be killed in a car accident. No, it was not an accident; she jumped, some whispered, stirring more morbid rumors about the deceased. Some pitied the minister who lost his position and was washed up to their village. Some pitied, most of all, his new wife. What a position, they said, to fill in for a dead wife, a beautiful one at that, and his first love. She was lucky, very lucky indeed to have a son, his only son.

Minister Jang continued his work without betraying a sign he knew of the rumors that set his village astir. He continued the sermons he had planned prior to the stories about his past, and continued the same attitude toward his congregants, always polite, if grave and aloof. The attendance in his church decreased a little, but not significantly, and little fluctuations now and then were to be expected. The road to faith entailed many turns and retreats, as Apostle Paul had plainly showed and explained. Such challenges would not buckle him. God had forgiven him. To his relief and pleasure, his young disciples clamored for more stories and songs and gleefully competed to answer his questions. Their attendance did not slacken.

Toward the end of August, as he waited for his congregation to gather for an evening service, the minister saw, to his surprise, Grandmother Lee coming to his church. She had never before come near his church, and he was quietly relieved at not having to deal with her, for he could not have mildly or meekly countenanced her foolish outpourings. She was also the culprit who had instigated the torments he had to endure recently. Did she feel a tinge of remorse? Why was she coming? He was to treat her as any newcomer, without undue interest and gentle greetings after the service. His prepared sermon was fortuitously appropriate, he thought.

He preached in his firm cadence how all is vain without love for fellow creatures, love for God, and love in divine fellowship. His words seemed to pierce each of his listeners, his two young daughters in the front row and his wife with his son, the faithful congregation that gathered near them, and his own heart. He was expounding how love thaws hatred and brings peace and harmony between neighbors, when Grandmother Lee stood up in the middle of the tent. She looked around her with a sneer at the corner of her wrinkled mouth and, as if to prove the falsity of it all, walked out of the church. Near the entrance, she stopped and gazed back toward the congregation.

"Tzz, tzz, he should get his house in order before sermoniz-ing," she growled, gesturing with strange forcefulness. "Tzz, tzz," she spat and turning around, trotted off.

Minister Jang had paused for a moment when Grandmother Lee got up, but he quickly collected himself and resumed the ser-mon. It was not unusual for a person to get up during the service for some emergency, or non-believers who drifted into it to re-move themselves for one reason or another, although people moved discreetly and strove to be non-disturbing on such occa-sions; it was not out of the ordinary. But as he continued, while he found his place in the sermon quickly enough, his cadence was altered. While it seemed as strong as before, it began to tremble and quivered ever so slightly. He hurriedly finished the sermon and took refuge in those moments the leaders of his con-gregation afforded him. They, without relying on him, guided the rest into strong, beautiful hymns.

This village on the hills of Sungbook, was it his reward for all the years he studied against his father's wishes? He had fol-lowed his heart and Christ. Was it all but pride, as so often said his own father, a tenant farmer for the same family his own fa-ther had served?

"Pine worms eat pine leaves. Pine worms, they live on pine trees," he mumbled day in and day out and turned on young Minister Jang, especially when he caught his youngest son with books at the wrong moments.

"You gonna to bring on wrath on you, you fool! Mark my words. Pine worms eat pines leaves. You seen anything differ-ent? Out, out! Go and look for yourself, you blockhead, tzz, tzz, tzz." At such times, it was his mother who brushed his father away and gave moments for young Minister Jang to lick his wounds. And he had persevered on with his books.

He married Sinyoung, a glorious beauty eleven years younger than he when he was starting out in a large church. He barely endured their wedding ceremony for he had the unreasonable fear that she would disappear or de-materialize before it was over. How many gods must have been jealous! She was young and more beautiful than any woman to whom he had been introduced, and upon seeing her, it was she whom he had to marry. They lived happily, or reasonably happily, so he had thought when one day when she appeared at his church dressed like a whore. Her scanty dresses revealed not only her arms and cleavage but also lapped against her white thighs; and her eyebrows were painted in darkest black, and her lips, bright blood red. Privately, if she had tormented him privately for infinitely different reasons, he would have endured. He would have endured, ignoring or trying to ignore her hysteria, bitter accusations, and childish antics. He would have cajoled, commanded, and demanded her to come to her senses and would have endured, if it had remained between only them. Once public, he could not break his own ultimatum and take her back as his good congregation had tried to persuade him. He abhorred vulgar compromises. His life could not be, or he would not let it be a tin pot soldered once too many. A few weeks after he had packed her suitcases and sent her away, she was found dead, hit by a train.

The approaching fall brought a clear blue sky unmolested by sultry heat, which cheered people. Dew began to descend at dusk a little earlier and lingered at dawn a little longer than before, while the leaves and grass thinned. The attendance at Minister Jang's church stayed about the same through the summer and fall. People in his village, having known Grandmother Lee all

35

their life, while stirred initially by her shocking words, rejected her conclusion. They also censured her appearance at his church. It was beyond common decency; and a sense of justice, which said that bygones were bygones, and nobody had any business in dredging them up, especially when the minister was trying to rebuild his life and had not harmed them. They prevailed over a few who would argue and split hairs over his competence and his influence as a minister. No one was required to attend his church, and Minister Jang and his family were to be left alone as long as they did not stir the village with any new shameful scandal. He also succeeded in finding a new location for his church for the coming winter. The Presbyterian Ministers Association for his district agreed to help him rent a hall in a church, two hills below from the village on the southern side of the Bookak Mountains.

The services in the new location were to begin in November, and Minister Jang planned to continue his work in the village until the day he was to dismantle his tent. A grave person, he got up earlier than anyone in the village for morning prayers and retired to bed only after it was impossible for him to contemplate one more line of the Holy Scriptures. But fear swelled in him at times and compelled him to reason constantly that he was saved.

God was on his side. The way he persevered indicated it. The way he found a new place of worship showed that He was pleased with him. The way he had studied, coming up to Seoul on his own and working through his school years, must have found pity in His eyes. These would not have been possible without His Grace. Yet his mind missed that something. Surely, he had the same God who gripped him when he was but a child and the same family that only a few months ago rallied him to ward off his renewed afflictions. But his mind was closing on him: he was trampled, ignored, and humiliated, and he required something else. Despite the signs of his recovery, or perhaps because of it, he was unhinged, and alone. In a stark open field, he was alone and could not remember how he got there.

With all his might, Minister Jang sought deliverance from his troubled mind and found peace most always during the early morning hours in his tent, as dawn ever so slowly illumed increasingly bare branches and hardening dirt. God did not forsake him. He would prevail. However, when he preached in the tent, before a congregation that began to dwindle as the days became colder, the cadence of his sermons, which he delivered with force and belief as he had done so many times, seemed to waver and dissipate in midair. His words did not reach the hearts before him, he knew, for surely they did not reach his own. He stole glances at his congregation and knew so well the panic in his wife's doleful face, and a solicitous smile, or was it a furtive sneer, on Youngmie's beautiful oval face.

On a day in late October, Minister Jang told his wife he would go on a retreat. He would pray for forty days and forty nights. He would come back fortified and blessed with love of God. He asked his wife to pack a small suitcase. When the leaves burned Korea's mountains red and yellow, Minister Jang sought a place for holy prayers deep inside the forest of Sulak, away from people and the temptations of food and water. He placed a cotton mat on the ground and knelt beneath the curving granite. Forty nights, forty days. God's love. He would not move until he prayed for forty days and forty nights. Pine worms, pine leaves, pine, and God's Grace. He would be marked, marked as His beloved.

Hikers found him prostrate on the top of a large granite cliff. They gave him water, brought him to warmth, and sought a doctor. When Minister Jang opened his eyes, they did not focus. His lips would not stay closed.

A Family

The wind pummeled his one window that faced the screeching mountains and hills behind his house. Mr. Kim lay unable to end incessant thoughts, which trailed one after another through the night. This winter was harsher than any he remembered although it could not in fact be worse than those during the war, or the ones in his hometown in North Pyongyang Province. His youth then must have spared him from knowing this kind of cold. It seeped through his very marrow.

It would be warm in Vietnam where his friend Hwang went to aid the military. Generous, Hwang warmed up especially to him when they worked at a construction site. They were from nearby villages in North Korea, sharing similar accents, gestures, and memories of distant places. Through hardships and new adventures, they could have had one another, had he followed Hwang.

But he was not free like him. He could not have left behind his wife and child, even if it meant a better future for them in the long run. When his friend first asked Kim to accompany him, he shivered with horror at the tempting possibility. But it was impossible. His wife was sick and his child, weak. He could not imagine leaving them behind, or how they would survive on the hills of Sungbook without him. Living here required much climbing and physical exertion. The money was tempting; the adventures he could scarcely let himself imagine; but he could not knowingly risk losing his family. Once was enough, more than enough. Mr. Kim wondered if his parents were still alive, whether his brothers and sisters had survived the war, and if they did, where they lived. He was thirteen when he lost them amid the mayhem that followed the retreating armies of the Allies and South Korea.

This winter was harsh, extremely harsh. He really needed to go out tomorrow and get some food. The sounds of the wind did not bode well. It was a shame he had no news from Hwang. Like him, Hwang must not like writing. What could he write back, even if he had gotten a letter from him? Could he have changed his fortune? The news said how valiantly the Koreans fought in Vietnam and earned great love and respect for their country. As any Korean would, they were honorably paying back some of the debt Korea owed to their allies. Kim did not doubt Hwang and others in Vietnam would do their utmost, far beyond the call of their duty. It was their once-in-a-lifetime chance, for Vietnam was also a ticket to America. His friend Hwang could be striking it rich in the Beautiful Country, while he could not buy food for his family.

The weather must thaw soon. He would then have more work. He could try construction sites and scour different villages, calling out for pots and pans in need of repair and exchanging metal scraps for sticks of taffy. He could also help in springtime moves and clean the outhouses. He could then afford something other than potatoes.

"Nanhee! Nanhee," barked Mrs. Kim as she woke from her nap after lunch. Nanhee did not leave a glass of water for her when she cleared the table away. Mrs. Kim pulled her body toward the hinged door that led to the kitchen. Pushing it open, she called out for Nanhee again.

"Yes! I'm coming Mother!" Mrs. Kim heard Nanhee shouting back to her calls. From the sound of her voice and the rustling noise her footsteps made, Mrs. Kim could guess how far Nanhee was from home.

Stupid little girl, thought Mrs. Kim. She was always disappearing now that the weather was warm. Heaven knew what she found so interesting on the empty hills behind their house. It was on the far western periphery of the village, where neither passersby nor romping children came near. Deep loneliness enclosed it. While she told herself that it was a blessing not to have any snooping neighbors nearby and that the Ahns a hill below were more than enough, Mrs. Kim keenly missed the company of others. And as she waited for Nanhee, each minute felt to her as if it were an eternity. She called for her daughter a few more times, getting angrier each time at Nanhee's slowness. She lacked a child's vivacity. She was inconsiderate, never as alert as she expected of her. It was a wonder how she bore such a child; she might as well be a stranger's child, thought Mrs. Kim, remembering how she was at Nanhee's age. All her life, she was supple, lively, and even brilliant – that is, until the disaster that struck her after Nanhee's birth. Hers was a cruel fate: her agility and gracefulness for Nanhee's dullness.

"Couldn't you have run faster?" Mrs. Kim barked, as Nanhee pulled the wicker door to their kitchen.

"Bring me some water please," added Mrs. Kim, calming herself.

"Yes, Mother," answered Nanhee, but did not move as her mother wished for her to quickly do.

"What's wrong?"

Nanhee brought out her fist from behind her back and showed a bunch of violets.

"Pretty. Aren't they pretty?" said Nanhee, still absorbed in those tiny flowers.

"Yes, yes they are. Now a glass of water, please," said Mrs. Kim, shifting her upper body to relieve the pressure on her left shoulder, which she had been leaning against the doorframe. Nanhee placed the violets just inside the doorsill and moved towards the water vat In a corner of the kitchen, out of Mrs. Kim's view.

The violets were exquisite in their purple hue. But even those petals that were not bruised from Nanhee's handling were sadly withered. She was only a child, thought Mrs. Kim. But more often she seemed a spirit. Absorbed for hours with leaves, flowers, berries, twigs, and dirt, Nanhee did not miss people. For that, Nanhee, her child, was lucky, thought Mrs. Kim. She was thankful.

"Don't scrape the wall, I've told you!" Mrs. Kim hollered when she heard the plastic gourd scratching the clay water pot.

"Yes Mother," Nanhee answered sweetly, lifting her upper body, which she had bent over the vat, stretching and on her toes. It was nearly as tall as she and huge in comparison to her slight body.

"Pour it carefully now. We don't want the dregs!" said Mrs. Kim. It was fortunate that she could not see Nanhee: she was unlikely to perform as she was told. After a few sips, Mrs. Kim handed Nanhee back the bowl of water.

It was musty and did not relieve Mrs. Kim's thirst. She craved for something else, a cucumber, a radish, a pear, something crunchy, succulent, and refreshing. She shook her head. It was a wonder how she could still hanker so even after such long hard years. It was strange. She pulled herself with her upper arms toward her bed and lay down.

Nanhee came in cautiously and closed the door after her. The afternoon light diffused in through the top part of the one window of their house and dimly lit the small room. Nanhee arranged the violets on the floor above her mother's pillow and lay next to her. Seeking her hand, her mother linked their fingers together, squeezing hers tightly. Nanhee muted instinctive cries of pain. She was not to provoke her mother. Shortly, she would slacken her hold. When Nanhee was smaller, she inevitably fidgeted and earned a round of her mother's rebuke. Now at the age of eight, she could lie as quietly as the violets she put beside her mother's pillow. It was easy, much preferable to rousing her mother's temper. She could also block out at times, without putting her hands to her ears, her mother's interminable lamentations and sickly groans, which, unfiltered, terrified her, as in the dreams where she was in free-fall.

Mr. Kim showed up at the Ahns' house in the late afternoon of April 3, 1971. He stood in the middle of the yard and asked awkwardly for the man of the house, the grandfather of the gaggle of children who were gripped by his appearance at their house. It was unusual that he should be at their house mid-afternoon, or to appear without his two buckets for water and a long pole for carrying them, or to ask for their grandfather when he almost always dealt with their big aunt, Mr. Ahn's oldest daughter-in-law. While an alert boy went inside to fetch the grandfather, Mrs. Ahn, who was in charge of the household by virtue of being the oldest woman in the house, appeared from the kitchen and provided shelter to the young children, who instinctively clustered about her. Cleared of them, Mr. Kim continued his awkward, dazed stance in the middle of the yard.

"Come in, come in," Mr. Ahn said, as he appeared from the inner room.

"No, thank you." Mr. Kim politely refused the invitation.

"My Nanhee is dead," he uttered, without looking at anything particular as everyone waited to hear the purpose of his unusual visit. All eyes ripped him in disbelief; time stopped. Each one struggled to haul off its onerous weight. The forlorn man in the middle looked inexpressively tender and frail.

"Malnutrition, malnutrition, the doctor said," Mr. Kim uttered, answering the unspoken question in everyone's mind. Mr.
Ahn came down from the foyer and stood nodding before him.

"We will take care of it," he said. "Take some rest. Take a
rest, and then go."

"Thank you. That is enough," Mr. Kim bowed and then turning, left behind him a wake of heavy silence.

Mr. Kim had not been alarmed a week ago when he found Nanhee lying asleep next to her mother when he returned from work.
She had always been a weak child and had a small appetite.
When she refused to sit up for dinner, his wife surmised that she
must be tired from roaming the hills for the violets. When
alarmed by her limpness, Mr. Kim dashed down the hills,
begged Dr. Jun to come to his house, and returned home with the
doctor, it was too late. Nanhee had stopped breathing. To her
dazed parents, the doctor said that it was malnutrition; she died
of it, he said. He then told them not to worry about his fees and
pressed Mr. Kim to visit him after the funeral. A sack of rice and
a bagful of groceries were delivered on that day to the Kims,
with a card from Dr. Jun. It indicated he was a servant of Jesus.

After Mr. Kim left her house, Mrs. Ahn was charged with
getting the help that her father-in-law had promised. She was the
oldest woman of the house, knew the village inside out, and
could most effectively elicit sympathy for the Kims. It was also
out of the question for Mr. Ahn to run errands from house to
house. She scurried the village most urgently, arousing or trying
to arouse pity and sympathy in her listeners. Despite her efforts,
she collected only a pittance. The neighbors who were most
sympathetic and to whom she could pitch the story to the fullest
had little to share. The neighbors who were better off, she could

44

visit only gingerly. They dared not find their heart for fear of being contaminated with misery and poverty; they feared their neighbors' envy and endless requests for help and were afraid to stoke unwelcome friendship. After her rounds, flushed from her exertion, Mrs. Ahn visited the Kims briefly and, with deep embarrassment, handed an envelope to Mr. Kim.

His wife comported better than Mr. Kim had feared. She suppressed her usual lamentations and reproaches. She did not seek pity. She led him to rest when he could not proceed after cleansing Nanhee on a folded sheet of hemp cloth. Leaning against a wall, Mr. Kim watched his Nanhee; she seemed to float upwards in the diffused dust that lit in the late sunlight coming in through the one window. His innards knotted in shame; his brain ceaselessly bubbled forth questions, further exhausting him. He craved numbness that would still him.

His wife broke the descending darkness by lighting their oil lamp.

"I will wrap her tomorrow," Mr. Kim said, wrenching himself away from his own thoughts.

"Yes," said his wife. She dragged herself toward a wall near the kitchen and retrieved two rice bowls, which were kept beneath a blanket to keep them warm. She then pushed them towards a small lacquer table in a corner of the room and then, having dragged herself toward it, uncovered the linen towel that kept the dust from the dishes.

"Mrs. Ahn brought these," she said.

Mr. Kim sat still despite his mind, which said he should get up and help her.

"It was my fault," her voice trailed and broke the silence that followed her last comment. He stayed still, resisting his mind, which said he should comfort her.

"It should have been me. I am the cripple," she said. Mr. Kim continued his silence despite the pity arising in him and the knowledge that he should deny her self-accusation.

He had indeed wondered why it was Nanhee, and not he or his wife. He had wondered whether she would have died, had her mother been more attentive. He knew his wife could have done more. She could have kept the house better despite her crippled leg. She should have been gentler, more loving toward their girl. None of that mattered. They were the survivors.

"I will finish it tomorrow," Mr. Kim said finally and said no more despite his mind, which said he should be nicer to his wife. Mrs. Kim nodded, tears running ceaselessly on her creased cheeks. She voiced none of her pitiful reproaches. She and her husband kept a silent vigil until they fell asleep.

Mr. Kim woke before dawn, followed by his wife.

"I will bury her this morning," he said "Yes," said his wife, agreeing implicitly that a longer vigil would be excessive for a child and given their situation. He carefully wrapped Nanhee in the hemp cloth and tied a rope about her feet and trunk. He could not continue and do the same for the head. Tears fogged his vision. Wiping her own her tears, his wife waited. She then led him aside, asking him to take a rest.

The morning was still early when Mr. Kim finished preparing Nanhee and went outside to gather his tools. The early sun-rays promised a brilliant spring day. He redirected his rising anger at the pitiless season, telling himself his life too neither stopped nor slowed. He gathered his pickax, shovel, and A-frame. When he returned to the kitchen, his wife had pulled herself to the doorsill and was waiting for him.

"I will bury her by the lilac tree," said Mr. Kim, laying down the A-frame and his tools.

She nodded. The old lilac on a hill beyond their home unfurled a canopy of purple lights each summer, delighting their child.

"Let me go with you," she pleaded.

"Y e s," Mr. Kim answered slowly, wondering how he would comply and whom he would carry first.

"I will go over there and first make the arrangement," he said.

Mr. Kim was enlarging a hole in the ground, which was harder than he had expected, when two sons of old Mr. Ahn bounded over, saying they were sorry for coming late. They had spotted him going up the hills when they were headed for his house. They quickly set to work. In silence, Mr. Kim accepted their help. He had not expected their appearance and did not know how to refuse their help without creating a scene.

"Now, that's enough," said Mr. Kim, when they had made a large enough grave. "I can do the rest. Thank you."

"We can help you. The coffin," said the older of the two.

"No, that won't be necessary. I will have to wait until my wife feels ready."

The brothers understood his desire to be left alone and said goodbye, bowing politely. He sat by the graveside and watched them roll down the hills. It was rude to send them away that way. So be it. He would not be naked again before his neighbors.

With a brief nod, Mr. Kim greeted his wife, who was hobbling about in the kitchen. She greeted him, avoiding his eyes. He had known, and she had known that he had known she could move, however haltingly and badly hobbling. They did not broach the subject after a series of her outbursts following their slow realization that the loss of movement in her left leg, which followed Nanhee's birth, was permanent. A show of surprise at seeing her in the kitchen, an encouragement or remorse, could unhinge her balance, Mr. Kim thought. Her litheness had been her hallmark before the pregnancy, and she had stubbornly refused to show herself in this new light. She had preserved or persevered to preserve her pride, a shard of it.

Wishing to give her space, Mr. Kim entered the room. A small table was before Nanhee's wrapped corpse. His wife handed him, without meeting his eyes, a bowl of rice and then a bowl of soup. He received them in the same manner and placed them on the table.

He felt keenly, without seeing, each movement his wife made as she climbed over the doorsill with inordinate difficulty, first settling her haunches on the sill on the strength of her upper arms, then pivoting to bring in her right leg, and then lifting and pulling up and in her wasted leg. She was risking a further loss of her pride and vanity, or the remains of which she had doggedly guarded. He could not blame her with the charge of outliving Nanhee.

Mr. Kim paid homage for the departed soul of Nanhee: circling sticks of incense above the food and bowing deeply, he invited it to accept the offerings and prayed for Nanhee's safe journey and well being in the next world. His wife performed her part sitting, and with his help. Afterwards, he carried his wife and sat her next to the gravesite. Despite the difficulty of climbing the hills with her in his arms, her breath and the heat from her emaciated body surprised and soothed his senses. He then carried his Nanhee. Her littleness and her coldness drove him nearly mad.

The sun, high up in the sky, beamed down brilliant April rays by the time the Kims returned home. Although she had sat silently next to the grave during the burial, Mrs. Kim burst into a wail when she returned to their empty room. After helping her to lie down, Mr. Kim went out. Make a river of tears, if you could, he said to her in his mind. He felt the heat of shame arising in him as he remembered how he had feared and resented the possibility of his wife losing herself in lamentation and hysteria.

Suppressing his shame and telling himself that it was for occasions such as this that man had tears and the capacity for lamentation, Mr. Kim began his plan to isolate his home. He gathered logs and cut small limbs of the trees on the hills to block off the footpath from the village to his house. Without the path, no one would come near or pass by his house on their way to the upper part of the stream below. He could reach the other parts of Seoul. The upper stream was shallow and had a plenty of steppingstones.

No one had any business coming near him. He did not need any of the miserable people in his neighborhood. Mal – nu – tri – ton, d-i–e-d of mal – nu – tri – ton, he had said. He bore himself naked, asking for their help. A fool, he was. It was pure folly. He believed in their decency, having known them as his neighbors all these years. Yes, their life was difficult too, but they would have found a way to scrape, rummage, squeeze, rake in more than a few bills and a sack of rice, if, if one of theirs died, if, if they had a modicum of respect for him. Misty eyed, he would not be. He was disabused of human decency.

Mr. Kim blocked off the passage by mid-afternoon. Without a pause, he began to redirect to his well the spring water that eventually reached the Anhs' well in their backyard. His well was unusable, for the amount of water from the forest had decreased over the years, while theirs was still full of cool, mountain water. Man was to till Nature for his benefits. It was madness to pay for buckets of water when he could have taken the matter in his hands.

The news of the blocked path spread quickly. Understanding it vaguely as his assertion to be left alone and in the light of his recent misfortune, the people of the village acquiesced without much comment. Few had ever approached the part of the hills beyond his house. Nothing useful or bountiful lay by its side. If one absolutely had to reach beyond it, he could re-climb the hills after descending the main road and re-crossing the stream further up from the one lane dirt road after crossing the metal bridge.

By the time Mrs. Ahn realized what was happening to her well, Mr. Kim's oddness had become old news. Loudly she broadcast his offense once she suspected his guilt. Tirelessly she complained, attempting to gain her listeners' sympathy, and to prove Mr. Kim's brazen ingratitude, she recounted all the little things she had done for him and his family. In the end, despite her anger, resentment, and longing for her old well, which was so full of cold, refreshing water that she had used it to refrigerate her many dishes, Mrs. Ahn could only acquiesce. Her father-in-law refused to make an issue of it. Given Mr. Kim's declaration that he was no longer part of the village, it was doubtful also what social pressures could work on him, and she could not stand sentinel over the water flow even if he were persuaded this time to restore it.

Mr. Kim busied himself with various jobs after severing his ties to the village, and when he was not working or searching for work, he carried out household tasks that were too difficult for his wife. Mrs. Kim stopped spending her days lying in the closed room and seemed to have found a new fount of energy. She cleaned and aired the room and always had dinner ready to serve him when he returned home. She jealously guarded a brood of chicks she made him buy for her and chronicled her adventures with them to his wonder and annoyance. If she missed other human beings, she did not express it. If her mind was full of Nanhee--as was his, she did not show it. Except for her severe limp, she seemed her old self, vivacious and even garrulous. Although he resolved several times to be understanding and to adjust his mood and attitude to her and her renewed demand for his affection, her chatter, and even her vivacity which was most exciting for him when they first met, often exasperated him.

By early summer, Mr. Kim resented not only this or that objectionable feature in his wife, but her relentless instinct for survival. He accused her in his mind. She ate enough to survive while her own daughter died of starvation. He tried to recall: she ate more than he, didn't she? Who knew what happened while he was out searching dumpsters? Whether they had only potatoes, whether they were hard to digest, and whether Nanhee ate little from birth, his wife had failed. His mother chewed food for him when he was ill. His wife could have done the same. She could have made Nanhee's food more palatable and more digestible. She should have force-fed her. She would have, if she applied her cruel instinct for survival, just a tiny bit of it, for his child. She should have risen up long before Nanhee's death. She had failed.

On a July evening, after crossing the stream below the hills and climbing a few steps towards home, Mr. Kim could not continue as if he were rooted in the spot. His body needed a wash and a rest. His wife would be waiting for him. His feet did not move forward. He sat on a patch of grass. A strong green smell of the grass soothed him. From there, he gazed at the small protruding

51

boulder in the stream. Dusky water ceaselessly foamed against it. His wife endeavored to start anew. He had acquiesced. It was right to avoid further pain, to let their wounds be. He sat there in a trance, not knowing what it was that he could not face.

Countless stars, some piercingly bright, some faint, speckled the summer sky when he woke up. He jolted up, directing himself toward home. He stopped. He was less than the faintest star. Who would find him, were he to disappear? He would go beyond this little corner of Seoul. He would be free.

His wife - she was selfish, always selfish. He dared to rip the veil of decency and to live only for himself and his family. Why the family? He did not sign up to live with a cripple for life when he took Yunja as his wife. She would survive. Without him. He would leave the accursed village. Why a remnant of decency? Feelings of exaltation buoyed him. He would join his friend Hwang in Vietnam. Possibilities were endless once he crossed the stream to the other side and did not look back. He would roam the world, see its wonders, taste its boundless offerings, and grasp some.

His feet did not move downhill. Instead they crept upward and kept up with the rising ground, which continuously became steeper. They then gained urgency.

First, familiarity guided his steps. Then he began to distinguish different shades and luminosity of the night. He echoed to the night's wild vibrations, insects trilling with reproaches, some, with subdued welcome. Relief and gladness enwrapped him when he made out the lump of his home. It was endearing. Beneath the expanse of the stars and the Milky Way, it was charming.

His wife had left the kitchen door ajar. He stepped in carefully and removed his shoes. Could he open the door to the room noiselessly? What would he say to his wife? He would tell her the truth: something about falling asleep and dreams of freedom. He opened the door and inched in. He could faintly distinguish his wife in a fetal position. He lay next to her.

The next morning, his wife was petulant, but did not ask him why he was late. He calmed her, telling her he had fallen asleep while taking a rest on his way home when Nanhee appeared and hurried him home. At the mention of their child, Mrs. Kim averted her face. He sought and held her hands. Neither struggled to suppress their welling tears or attempted to regain their composure.

After breakfast, Mr. Kim steadied his wife's gait as they walked up the hills to Nanhee's tomb. It was their first visit together since the day of the burial. The purple scent of the lilac was long gone. Instead, flush green leaves threw undulating shadows toward Nanhee's lush tomb. They tidied their child's home, giving it a haircut and were silent in their memories of Nanhee.

The Horizon

In the spring when Sungil came, I was sitting on the stepping-stone to the entrance to our living room, watching Sungwoon, my then youngest brother. With a stick, he was poking around a stone buried in the hard dirt. The very top that Sungwoon first spied was smooth and white; it promised to be a real find. But, it went a lot deeper than the tiny top seemed to indicate, and Sungwoon was digging about it a long time when our grandmother slid open a door from the main room and called out.

"Sunhee, go and fetch Aunt Oh. Quick! Don't fall!"

Auntie Oh lived one hill below us and was called whenever women in our village gave birth. My older sister Sunja was at school, so I was watching Sungwoon, and it fell on me to fetch her. I have two older brothers too, the oldest, Sungshik and the younger one, Sungkoo. They were always busy with studying: Father wished them to finish high school and then get scholarships, and besides the boys were not supposed to go into the kitchen and get hands wet. So my sister and I were the ones who helped out at home, and mostly I, when she was at school.

I ran down to Auntie Oh's house and shouted for her as I pushed her gate.

"I am coming! One moment! You go and tell them I am coming," she hollered, hurrying out of the kitchen.

I darted toward home and glanced behind now and then to make sure Auntie Oh with her large brown bag was not too far behind. She was taller and bigger than most of the uncles in our village and had a way of heaving as she lumbered up and down the hills of our village. She was goodhearted; you felt safe and warm when she was near you, like when you have your good mother about you. Shortly after she entered the main room, my grandmother came out.

54

"Out, out and play. And don't let Sungwoon cry." She hustled us out on her way to the kitchen.

Sungwoon had not yet succeeded in unearthing the stone; it was no small pebble as it first looked from its shiny white top. He refused to budge, ignoring my efforts to move him until Grandmother, peeking out from the kitchen, scolded us roundly to be out. I began to pull him. He flung the stick down and followed. It was early afternoon, and the streets were quiet. I did not wish to be far from our house, for it did not seem right to be out and playing when Mother was sick and a new baby was coming. I sat by the steppingstone to our gate, hoping our grandmother would call us in soon.

Sungwoon found another stick and started to dig again, this time, around the bottom of our steppingstone. He scraped the dirt around it and patted the ground about it neat and even. I scooped up the fine dirt he created and moved it away from our house. I liked the feel of the fine dirt slipping between my fingers. When Sungwoon neatly edged all around the steppingstone, he began to dig about the bottom of our sidewall. I stopped him. It could go on forever, and I did not wish to keep on clearing the dirt he scratched out. We would have more fun at Ayoung's house, I told him.

Ayoung was my best friend. She was the only child at her house and was usually alone when she did not play with her friends. Her mother was always at work, and her father, often absent from home. When we got to her house, two blocks from our house in the direction of the mountains, she was killing flies in her yard. She had heard from the radio that they caused all kinds of disease. You could see it was true because they sat on your food with the same tiny fuzzy feet after buzzing about and sitting on rotting garbage and dung. Ayoung had two more fly swatters, so I did not have to sit and wait my turn when I was a lot better than Sungwoon, and even better than Ayoung at catching flies. With fly swatters in our hands, we ran about her yard.

The radio was always on at Ayoung's home, keeping her company until her mother came home. She heard lots of things from it and often told me what she heard. Once when we were playing rock-paper-scissors at her house, a man with a deep voice said that ignorant people were chopping down the trees and ruining Korea's mountains. New laws would punish them severely, he said. I was gripped with fear, for my father often went to the mountains early at dawn for firewood. But I sat quietly until my panic subsided. I did not tell Ayoung what was wrong: I did not want her to look down on us; and if I ran home and told my mother what he said, as I first felt like doing when I heard him, she would be upset with me, I thought. So I kept quiet and thought about what the man said. It was true my father did not have much schooling. It was also true that you needed fire in winter and even in summer to cook rice, and sometimes you just did not have any charcoal bricks. The man on the radio was very smart, but did not tell the whole story. I did not like him.

When we were chasing a host of black flies, some, shiny black, and others dull and black, we noticed occasionally colorful ones gleaming green and gold.

"They must be western flies. Much worse than the black ones," said Ayoung.

"Let's kill them first!" I shouted. Without a peep, each of us pursued those bright colored flies harder than the black ones and even let go some easy black ones.

Everyone knew the westerners were bad, like the American who came after my aunt Miyoung, my mother's sister. She used to visit us once in a while with bags of groceries, and when she came, she looked like a movie star. One day she came home all tired, and shortly afterwards, the American came with a piece of paper, showing it to anyone who would help him to find her. Father was at home, and she dared not invite him to our house where everything was stone silent. She met him on the street, a block down the main crossroads. Ayoung and I, and all the other kids who saw him coming to our village watched them. They talked fast, and we tried to decipher what sounded like "shella, shella, shella" in a singsong way in a language which we figured must be English.

He must have been bad. Aunt Miyoung came to us sick and blue, and she spoke furiously, without giving him a moment to respond, and he kept trying to calm her. I was sure she was angry with him for coming after her like that. When the American left, Aunt Miyoung looked pale as a passing moon. In our house, not a mouse stirred. She must have cried all night. When I saw her leaving our house the next day, her eyes and face were all puffed up, even though she tried to make herself look pretty. I had a feeling that she might not visit us for a long time. She dared not greet Father before leaving us.

When countless dead flies were scattered all over the yard, we took a pause. We were thirsty. Ayoung picked up an orange plastic gourd, which was laid upside down next to the faucet in her washstand. Her house was one of the few in our village that had city water. She rinsed the gourd and filled it with water. We sat on the steppingstone that led to Ayoung's living room and passed it around.

"I will have another brother," I said to Ayoung. "Auntie Oh is at our house. Our grandmother told us to stay out. We can go back when our sister Sunja comes home from school."

"Boy, your mom can really pop out kids. Pop, pop,"

"Pop, pop, pop," Sungwoon followed Ayoung.

"Be quiet!" I yelled at him. I should have yelled at Ayoung, but I was a chicken, afraid to annoy her. He should have had better sense than to imitate her although I am sure neither meant any disrespect for my mother.

"My mother's belly looked like this," I said, drawing out a large belly as big as three watermelons.

"My grandmother says it will be a boy. When the belly stays up like this, it's a boy, she said. I will have four brothers."

"Is that good for you?" asked Ayoung.

I looked at her puzzled.

"I mean, your grandmother is happy. She loves boys. Look at how she is to your brothers, not at all like how she is to you. But what's that to you?" she said.

"Why, that means we will all be happy. We will have rice cake and hang large red peppers at the gate. Everyone knows boys are better than girls!"

Ayoung was smart, but she could be very strangely dumb. She must be still angry with my grandmother, I thought. She yelled at her the other day when she came to our house looking for me. I had spilt the rice I was washing for dinner, and my grandmother was super-angry when Ayoung entered our gate. She saw her yanking my hair. She looked horrified.

"You're always calling on Sunhee. She is busy. Can't you see?" my grandmother scowled at her too. Ayoung's eyes darted, from me to Grandmother and to the grains. I could not keep them from slipping through my fingers. I avoided meeting Ayoung's eyes. I was embarrassed, for me, for my grandmother, and for the spilt rice. Ayoung ran out of our gate, and that was the last time she was at our house.

"My grandmother isn't always mean," I said. She hollered at me often, but did not often slap me, and yanked my hair even less. Even Mother sometimes did that when I did something really stupid and made a big mess. My grandmother was not bad.

58

"I know," said Ayoung. "Like the last time when she gave us the rice cake."

That was a few weeks ago when Grandmother brought home a first batch of mugwort from the valleys and made green rice cakes that made the whole house smell green and peaceful.

"She also shows me how to embroider," I said, proud of my grandmother. She taught me how to sew, knit, and embroider as she did the odd jobs Mother brought home. She was busy with housework, Sister Sunja was at school, and I was too little to be of any real help.

"You are lucky," said Ayoung.

That was for sure, I thought. She had no grandmother who showed her how to do anything. Her parents were from North Korea, and that made her family very small.

"Anyway, do you want to catch more flies or what?" asked Ayoung.

"Let's go down to the stream." I did not wish to miss my sister on her way from school.

We ran down the hills and went to the shallow parts of the stream, further down from the bridge that connected our hills to the dirt road. Water sparkled and gurgled as it further smoothed the rocks by which Mother did our laundry when the weather was warm. Ayoung and I looked for smooth white pebbles, and some brown ones too. Sungwoon collected large stones and began building a fortress.

The following spring, Ayoung and I started school. I was in Miss Lee's class and she was in Miss Kim's class. I was excited to be a student at Sungbook Elementary School. It had a real playground, seesaws made of handsome wood, shiny metal slides, and a colorful, red, blue, green, and yellow, jungle gym. I was also proud to have my own schoolbooks. My sister helped me to cover them with glossy calendar sheets so that the white side showed when we finished wrapping them. She then wrote the subject name and my name on the front cover of each book in her beautiful handwriting. By then she had finished school and was helping Mother at home. She was also the one who took Ayoung and me to school to make sure that we were registered. That was a sad day for Ayoung.

We ran down our hills and crossed the stream. We were excited to see the school for the first time. The whole school was buoyant and festooned with ribbons and flags. A crowd of clean, good-looking people filled the school's large ground. We were to check our names on the bulletin boards that hung from the walls of the buildings. First, my sister looked for my name and found it right away. She then started to help Ayoung, who had not yet found her name. My sister could not find it either. We began scanning the boards with care, several times, hoping we were making a mistake and praying we would find it soon. The afternoon sun beat down on us, and we were hot, exhausted and ate more than our share of dirt that rose from the ground. Ayoung began to whimper. I felt bad for her. She wanted to be a student as much as I did, I was sure.

"Your father can come tomorrow and see the principal. I am sure it's just a mistake," my sister said to Ayoung. She burst into tears and made us the center of attention of the fancy mothers and children, who watched us with wonder. I felt embarrassed even though I tried not to show it. My sister tried to calm Ayoung.

"I am sure it's just a mistake. When your father comes," she was saying, when Ayoung blurted, blubbering and wiping her face with the back of her hands,

"My mom has to come. They had a big fight last night. He won't be home!"

I had more faith in her mother than her father. She was mean and scolded anyone who got in her way, like the hen that pecked away at my bun when I was little and in her way. Ayoung's mother got things done; her father was altogether different, gentle and quiet. But she always said nice things about him: how he used to be and how he spoke many languages. I never heard him speak any language other than Korean, very little of it too; I could not see what good it was if he could not help his family.

"I am sure your mother can fix it," I said, shaking off my thoughts about her father and remembering her mother. She did not make me feel warm like Auntie Oh, but I was sure she could do anything she wanted to.

"Sunhee is right," my sister said. "Your mother, she will make sure you will go to school, won't she? As soon as she sees the principal, she will fix it, right?"

Ayoung nodded. Sure enough, she came running to our house the next day to tell me that she could go school. Her mother found her name right away as soon as she got to school, she said.

In the beginning, I loved school, like Ayoung. We went to it together and came back together. But soon I didn't care for it as much. Ayoung started to stay after school with some of the other smart students in her class, decorating their classroom, studying extra, and helping out their teacher. Miss Lee did the same with the smart students in my class, and I, like my grandmother said, was not smart. So we began coming home at different times. We then went to school separately as I began to stay home more often, after my sister went to live in a rich family's house.

Sister Sunja left home during my first summer vacation. I watched Sungwoon while Mother, carrying little Sungil on her back, took her to the house downtown. Father had been working on a road near the Han River all that spring and summer, but Mother said he was getting old and not as strong as other, younger men. It would be better for Sister to live in a rich aunt's house, she said. She would help the aunt as she helped Mother at home. I do not think my sister wanted to go although she knew she had to. Sometimes you just did what you had to. At least she was going downtown. I had heard that it was fabulous: countless beautiful stores, big wide streets, and fancy people. Could I one day visit my sister? Would she show me glamorous Myong-dong? I wondered, but did not voice my thoughts, for even though I wasn't smart, I wasn't so dumb as to utter such silly things and stoke my grandmother's wrath.

That winter, Mother often made flour-drop soup. I loved the chewy dough in anchovy broth. She made the best flour-drop soup. On one late October day, Ayoung came to play with me, and Mother gave her a bowl of it. After that she kept coming to our house about dinnertime until Mother became annoyed and gave her a mean look. That day, she left before our dinner, although she stayed for a little while and helped me feed little Sungil. I was sure she loved the soup as much as I did and that her mother never made it.

That winter I got into big trouble with Father. I was not careful. One day in late November, after he had started to stay inside lying on the thick blankets on the warmest part where the heat from the kitchen was the strongest, he motioned toward me to hand him his cigarette pack.

"It's empty father," I said and went back to threading pretty little beads for a job my mother had brought home.

Father lay back, sighing. A few moments later, he said again, "Sunhee, bring me a cigarette!"

While I was mute, confused and not knowing what to say, Mother, coming in from the kitchen with a kettle of barley tea, told me to run down to Mrs. Han's shop down by the stream. She hated asking for more credit, and it was then I got the idea to collect cigarette butts and rolled out new ones in pieces of newspaper.

When Father again asked for a cigarette a couple of days later, and none was available, I handed to him the ones I had rolled. Father turned white and raged.

"Who told you? Who, to do this?" he thundered and hurled the cigarettes. Fits of coughing stopped him. I froze. Brother Sungkoo, who was studying in his room across the main room, came running, as did Mother from the kitchen. Sungkoo helped him to lie back down. Mother said I was only a child and that I did not know what I was doing. I was so scared. He had never yelled at me like that. Mother sent Sungkoo down to the corner store. I picked up the cigarette mess, wiped the floor, washed the rag, and sat by the hearth in the kitchen. I liked the warmth in it and being near to Mother. When she finished kneading the flour dough, she let me help her make round dollops and drop them into the boiling broth.

"Father does not want you to touch the cigarette butts; if you want, you can leave them here; he won't be angry with you," she said.

I nodded. I loved my mother.

Father became very sick that winter. In mid-December, when his coughing got worse, Mother sent me to borrow some rice from Auntie Oh. He needed to eat something better than soup, something like rice porridge. Under the dim light bulb in her kitchen, Auntie Oh counted cups of rice. ". . . three, four, five ...." The grains first clanged the tin pot I was holding and then made softer, duller sounds, which I wished would just continue. She stopped at twelve.

"Thank you. My mother said she will pay you back shortly," I bowed and ran up the hill.

That winter, Grandmother and I were busy making beads for fancy sweaters that went to America. But most of the money Mother had that winter must have come from Sister Sunja, even though her visits became less and less frequent. When she initially came home for a visit of two hours or so, Mother always asked the same questions. "Do they treat you right?" "Are you eating enough?" My sister always answered the same, in her soft, quiet way, "yes, mother". After her visits, thoughts would swirl in my head as I tried to lie still and fall asleep. I wondered whether she envied Sister Mija, the beautiful daughter of Auntie Oh, who was a student at a middle school. She wore school uniforms with white collars that framed her beautiful, milky face.

I wished secretly I too would wear such uniforms when I got older. I was not a good student and could not figure out how Mother would buy me such ones, for although Brother Sungshik would have graduated from high school, Brother Sungkoo would still be in school, and Sungwoon was to start elementary school. Regardless, I wanted to wear the uniforms, and Sister Sunja must have felt so too. But she looked just tired and quiet, and after her visits my mind kept spinning about things that were not true, wondering what it would be like if Father were not sick, if he worked in the police station like Jeeyoung's father, or if aunt Miyoung could still visit our house.

It was pointless to wish for things that were not true. It would be like Simchung wishing for something different: a mother, or a father who was not blind. But then, she would not have been her. Look at Simchung. She sold herself for three hundred cups of rice for her father's eyesight. It was pointless to wonder what would have happened if she were rich, if her father were not blind, or if he had not promised Buddha so much rice for his sight. But I could not stop my mind from going round and round about things that were not true.

After such nights, I would wake up very tired and would be glad when Mother said I was to stay home and help her. I would not have been able to follow Miss Lee's instructions. I was one of the worst students, so I sat in the last row, far from the heater. I did not like everyone knowing that I was not smart, and I was glad that Ayoung was not in my class although our eyes met once when my classroom door was slightly ajar and I was in my seat as she passed by.

When Miss Lee was explaining in the front of the classroom, I wondered how some of my classmates could remember and recite so many of the things she said. It was not fair that some people were smarter than others. Sometimes I watched my classmates, deciding which ones were pretty, which ones were rich, and whether I liked any of them. Some were loud and always knew the answers. They were the smart ones. I did not like them. Even Ayoung had that air. But she knew I was better than her in other things, like finding mugwort. Before the new houses and roads were built on the opposite mountains, I had shown her how to find them, but she had a hard time telling them apart from similar looking weeds. I was also better at knitting, embroidering, and threading beads. When I showed her how to knit, she kept tripping the needles and lost the loops. Yet, she was one of the best students, and the teachers liked her, unlike me.

The following spring, I stopped going to school. My tuition had been overdue from the previous fall, and I often sat in the hallway next to the principal's office with the other students whose tuitions were also not paid. One day the principal gave me a note to take home before the real spring set in. He wanted to see my parents, but Mother said there was no point in her meeting him

65

since she could not make money from stone. I stopped going to school after that.

I was rubbing a shirt on a flat stone by the stream like my mother was doing, when Ayoung saw us on her way from school. She looked more excited than usual and beamed at me. We had not seen each other for a long time. She came down from the road, and I stood up to greet her.

"Hello, Auntie, didn't Sunhee go school today?" greeted Ayoung.

"No, she did not," answered Mother, pausing the wash and pulling me close to her bosom. Ayoung looked exceptionally happy.

"Tomorrow is the school picnic! She will go to the picnic, right, Auntie?" My mother held me tightly. Neither of us answered her. Looking puzzled, Ayoung stood gazing at me, and then my mother.

"We are going to the Palace. There will be -" she stopped when mother turned to continue the wash and I made a half turn. That was the last time I saw Ayoung.

I would have liked to have gone to the picnic, but kept quiet. I had gone to the previous fall's picnic to the same palace. I walked on the large palace ground and saw its numerous gardens, gates, buildings, and sweeping pines. Some of them were hundreds of years old, the signs said. Following my classmates and Miss Lee, I also peeked into different rooms, each of which had a panel above the door that told the visitors what they were seeing in large black Chinese characters. I could not read them or hear through the noise other students were making any of the teacher's explanations. The old buildings did not have much to do with me.

On one side of the palace, there were rides and a zoo. The roller coaster and merry-go-round looked fun, but I did not ride

66

them. The animals stank. The tigers drew the largest crowd, but they looked bored and stayed away from us, except one that growled at us. Some students made faces at it, and a few boys poked sticks through the metal bars of the cage. The tiger snarled, swung its paws, and struck the metal bars instead. The boys were tickled and taunted it more. I did not like the zoo.

The only thing I really liked at the picnic was the lunchbox my mother packed for me: pieces of *kimbap*, candies, and a juice box. I loved the *kimbap*: seasoned white rice stuffed with spinach, carrot, yellow radish, and sausage, all wrapped in a roasted sheet of seaweed. Mother sliced the roll to bite sized pieces. The feast of their colors - white, black, green, orange, yellow, and brown - and their taste told me it was a special day. I would never get tired of eating them. I could have the same lunchbox if Mother was happy and Father became healthy again. I did not have to go to the picnic. I would not miss much.

When that spring was ending and the weather was turning hot, I went to live with Auntie Chu in Suhjoo. She was a distant relative of my father and owned a restaurant. I helped out in the kitchen, washing dishes, peeling garlic and onions, and trimming vegetables.

Suhjoo is in Cholla Province by the Yellow Sea, far from Seoul. When I saw the sea for the first time, I remembered the stories Miss Lee told the class before our first summer vacation. In her stories, children visited museums, parks, and grandparents during the vacation. In one story, the children went to the beach. They swam, built sand castles, and collected seashells. She showed us pictures of the beach dotted with colorful umbrellas. She called the line where the sky met the sea the horizon.

I liked the word. Horizon. I imagined it open blueness. She then told us our summer assignment: keep a journal. My heart sank. I would again fail to do my homework, for I would not do any of those activities I was supposed to. I did not keep a journal.

Now I could tell her how the horizon looked in early mornings and late evenings. I could tell her the colors of the sand when people crowded under the sun or when there was no one but the wind. I could also tell her what I liked best was the white foam that kept running towards the beach, spreading itself like countless fingers. As it washes away, it leaves behind countless bubbly holes. Then the creatures underneath are happy. I am lucky. I got to see the open sea before I was ten. I am sure Ayoung still does not know how the real horizon looks.

Mr. Han

I have sired four children, that is, at least four children claim my lineage. How does a man ever know if he has not sired one or two unbeknown to him? Of course, there are those who know only one, only one all through their life. They call it purity, virginity, things you believe in your cradle, in your youth of bright sunshine, not knowing your eyes are being smeared and narrowed, not knowing your ears are being hemmed and channeled. They are men of limited means, men of stunted souls, quite different from me, or from what I was. You have to know, a while back before I landed beneath the hills of Sungbook, I was the dandiest of men, cultured and better looking than any of Korea's top movie stars. That's another story.

As I was saying, four youngsters claim my parentage. "Claim" is the word, because, again, how would a man ever know if the thing that issues from his woman is truly his? Only she may know it for certain and at times even she may not know and claim it god-sent. Not that I doubt my poor wife's virtue. Well, my wife isn't really poor. I mean, there are many, numerous, countless like the sand on the beach who are as poor as she, and poorer. That is one thing Jesus said which was correct. The poor were before him and will always be. Of course, that doesn't really help when you are poor, especially when you had big, rich dreams. I am sure she never had dreamt she would end up here. She was a pretty little thing from a family of wealth and connections. That was before the war, well before all was washed away. Besides, who achieves all the beauty and success the young envision? Little accidents, nodding your head at the wrong time, walking next to the wrong person, events so trivial you don't even notice, histories that sweep mankind, empires whirling in smaller ones in their grand ambition, and your unalterable birth, events so far beyond your reach that you just stare open-mouthed, these unhinge and whisk you right along with untold millions and wedge all right into a quagmire.

You struggle. You want more. This is not you, you say. A mistake, you say. You are still all the things that you dreamed for yourself. You deserve it all, you claim, at least a good part of it all that was once yours, until years pass and you are still in a quagmire and can no longer say even in jest that you are still young. You shy away from the old pictures that show a strange youth grinning widely, staring straight into the camera.

Your heart still clamors. It clamors for the beauty that your mind had once spawned on the fables you indiscriminately gobbled up. You refuse to see where you are, preferring the haze. Yet, once in a while you glimpse - inevitable it is - and descry the odds and ends that accumulated about you. You would keep few, only a few, a very, very few, if any, if you had the courage. This is how I see it, at least on this morning of my forty-eighth birthday, as my thoughts wander while I lie on a cot inside a windowless hovel across from what was once a pristine stream beneath the hills, which must have once been an enviable green.

I do not mean to complain. The poor had to move somewhere, all those cramming to Seoul for a piece of its glamour; when the stream turned to a sewer, they had to pave it over, unless they wanted to beautify this corner of Seoul, which is pure nonsense. And this room isn't so bad. Next to my cot where I spend my days are a television, a radio, a fan, and a small table on which my wife keeps her hairpins, cosmetics, and whatnot. Across the room is a handsome dresser, made from chestnut wood and hand engraved, a relic from our old days. Here comes my wife of twenty some years. I close my eyes.

"Husband, I brought your medicine. The pharmacist says you must follow the directions. Three times a day."

70

She places a tin tray near my pillow. I do not wish to make the effort to stir and acknowledge her.

"Husband, you are not sleeping, are you? You have to take it! They say you can get better."

My wife sighs deeply. Poor soul. She waits.

We were married in 1948. She was nineteen. I was twenty-two, back from Japan, re-enrolled in a local university, and thinking of going to America when my mother suggested that I marry this girl from a good family. It was silly, even barbaric, the old match making, I had thought. I was a modern man. I had a fine, Japanese girl in Tokyo. Who but an ox would marry a simple Korean girl? Well, I married her, and this woman gave me four children.

I push down on my elbows and try to sit up. My wife takes the cue and gives me her arms. She takes the medicine packet from the tray and unfolds it. The thin onion paper crinkles. She gathers the white powder along its center crease and hands it to me. I slide the bitter medicine on my tongue and chase it with water.

How many men must have taken medicine, knowing fully they would not get well? The doctors say my tuberculosis is stabilizing, or at least that's what the one I saw the last time said. I see them off and on at the beck and call of money. When my wife gets some, she gets hopeful and nags me to see them until I do. The doctors have been saying I could be cured ever since, if I heeded their advice. Take medicine and eat well. I obey them and then get sidetracked. What do they really know? They dispense confidence, boosted by diplomas, their colleagues' courtesy, obsequious subordinates, the adoration of their mothers, wives, daughters, and old men, and their patients' fear and ignorance. Admirable, but, what do they really know? Could a doctor, whether a consummate physician deserving veneration, an

71

earnest novice full of best wishes, or a simpleton trapped in physician's accoutrements, re-fasten a splintered soul? Let them exude confidence. Let them dispense confidence! The world needs it. A broken soul knows only time will give him a rest.

My wife hands me a wet towel. I use it to wipe off water and traces of powder from my lips.

"Will you go for a walk, husband?" she asks. I am silent.

"It's a nice day for a walk," she insists. She has got it into her head that it would be good for me to go out today.

Why not, who knows if she is not right, think I.

"Hhm. I suppose. I could visit Mr. Suh, I suppose," I say.

I had helped Suh a few times when things were different. He is the only one who still keeps up with me, that is, he looks me up once or twice a year. My wife's face lights up at my mention of him. She heaps praises upon him. You would think he was a saint - all because he brought us a case of apples last fall. He receives them yearly from his family down in Kyongsang Province. My wife then checks herself, suspicious that I might change my mind. She hurriedly exits my room and says she will get hot water ready.

She must have received a letter from Sunmie. She treats me better and performs the role of a dutiful wife caring for a sick husband more earnestly when she receives a letter from our oldest child in Vietnam. The money Sunmie sends from Vietnam oils her family here. Poor child. I had never dreamed of living off a child's earnings. The modern man in me retches at the idea. I had argued and expounded, heatedly, earnestly, and confidently that only the ignorant feed upon their young. Here I am, filching the life of my poor child, who obediently carries out, bovine like, the supposed duties of daughters in legends that were fed to her when she was but a toddler, or before, perhaps long before she was conceived.

72

At a quarter to eleven, I walk down the wide, empty asphalt road. It is not the Champs Elysees one dreams of when one is young, or even the avenues by the old palaces lined with old plane trees. An empty bus idles at the forlorn terminal. I am in no hurry. I will walk to a telephone booth. I have never initiated contact with my old acquaintances since I became ill, wishing to spare them feelings of guilt and embarrassment. I know well enough the limits of our good intentions before a persistent situation that defies an easy solution.

Despite dirt and poverty that assault my eyes, the day is glorious, the sky, high and clear, the air, crisp and cool. It is a perfect day of the early fall, Korea's best season - a much waited and yearned for respite after sultry August.

I sit in a restaurant, one of those that crowd the back alleys near the American embassy where Suh works. He dispenses fear and sympathy to those who line up to meet him with high, bursting hopes for the Beautiful Country and with inexpressible fear of anyone who could block their aspirations. He used to work in one of the translation offices that throng about the embassy, assembling documents, fingerprints, blood tests, pictures, whatever America and its embassy say Korea's hope surfeited would-be-emigrants must show. It's a circus, all the things that America demands from them, of their war-torn family registers and poverty-stricken bellies. Of course these would conjure up magical men in cubicles who fill in the forms, assemble, translate, and create identities, exhorting, allaying, and colluding with their ignorant and not-so-ignorant clients, the sly and the not-so-sly.

Suh comes in hurriedly twenty minutes later than the time he had mentioned over the telephone. He has a colleague with him.

"Brother, it has been so long! Did you order?" He is full of nervous energy.

"Miss, Miss. Here!" he calls out to the serving girl.

"Look at this, so late. I couldn't get out. It was crazy right before I was about to leave. They couldn't find a file for a family that came up from Mokpo. Well, they will have to wait until it shows up. Here, this is Mr. Shin. He is new in my section. And here is Mr. Han. We go back a long time. Fifteen, twenty years?"

We exchange polite greetings. Suh updates me on the news of our old friends, gingerly, gently inquires about my wife and children, and exchanges shoptalk with Shin. I try to be non-intrusive, commending him for his prudence and ability to bring along Shin, a young man in his early thirties. Suh did not have a reason to expect my call and must be anxious that I might ask an embarrassing favor. But he behaves bravely, fronting a calm exterior, eschewing sticky issues, social, political, or economic, which could turn dangerous when the students and Park are at each other again. And he is not a blockhead to bring up the topics of money and health before an impecunious and sick acquaintance. Little is left after these off-limits, and the conversation stalls and jerks, but Suh admirably maneuvers without touching off any of the minefields. His ears twitch curiously and turn crimson.

We part. I like him. Nothing to be offended. We have faded memories of our old bravado. I am relieved to part from my old ghost. Leaving the restaurant, I continue down the back alleys of the restaurants, antique shops, grimy cafes, hardware stores, and jewelry shops. I revisit each word of Suh. For a person like me, unused to meeting others, a small encounter like this unlocks tsunamis of emotion.

I do not envy Suh's ability to hold on to his job and respectability, although I should tip my hat to his achievement. It's no mean feat to grip your way through the quicksand that followed the war, fevers of democracy, the Revolution of April Nine-teenth, the Coup of May Sixteenth, assassinations, market crashes, botched elections, demonstrations, prisons, and massa-cres. To bury himself deep in his business, and forage food and clothing for his children, that is by no means a small little task. I could never get used to the office, being tied to a desk and having to respond to the whims of a boss and the politics that fouled even my little cubicle; the endless shuffling and filing of papers, all superbly important for a short span and then gather-ing dust as they slowly decay until, if ever, a whippersnapper mistakes a few fading ink blots for an extremely important key to unlock threatening sewage.

I craved beauty. I wanted to live before my heart dried sap-less and I became a useless block of meat. I wanted to live - for me. Well, the truth was that I was born rich and never worried about money until it all disappeared. And I found myself in ever diminishing roles, job after job, and in the end, became unable to get one.

I enter Jongro; the day is still young. I set my steps towards Pa-goda Park. Peddlers hawk cheap food and candies. Pigeons dart after crumbs, dirty and mean enough to not fear man. A crowd of men crane their necks around the chess players. They are idlers, like me, no, better than me - they seek relief in the com-pany of others. I toss a coin and receive a newspaper from a grimy boy. The headlines tell the same old stories - student demonstrations, the military police at the gates of universities, petitions of silver tongued leaders of the opposition, editorials backing the regime, expounding the need for tougher national emergency laws in view of the newly unearthed Communist sympathizers, and a new poem by Park's mouthpiece. The same old twists and turns after glorious April Nineteenth; the same old, except we now have Park and his cronies in place of those who had propped up that doddering old man and new crops of the young, young and foolish and brave enough to dream justice and eager to prove their mettle.

I lost my money before I learned its value, a casualty of a string of misjudgments amid the coup of May Sixteenth and the financial upheavals finagled to secure pots of gold for Park's presidency. The fact that my brother was an idealist and defected to the North did not help either. Blacklisted, I could not find work even for a position that barely required education. Not that I blame my brother. He could not sit still, fired up with passion for a just Korea. Why not, when anyone who had heart enough to feel, was pulled to the left, to the right, and saw visions of justice, equity, and a grandiose new Korea. I understand him. Only I would not have exchanged my life and comfort for some ideology, be it communism, nationalism, or Americanism. I would rather savor the fruits of civilization, the art, the music, and beautiful women. I would be as happy as a fat tortoise in a forgotten forest.

Likely the employers also sensed that I did not truly want their job. Nevertheless, I would have liked to continue to wear an impeccable white shirt and stroll like a gentleman. I would have liked to reject offers rather than be rejected. I heard many excuses, reasons, and silences. Shall I count the ways to bury a man alive?

I should be thankful, though, that I did not meet the fate of those the KCIA took its time and energy to whisk to the rooms beneath Southern Mountain. They must have known I was harmless, that I could not be worked up about any ideology. I am not a believer. My wife saw the glimpse of the man she married only when she was carrying her fourth child. As we were sinking, she begged, scraped, screamed, and screeched, in short anything she could do to wring enough to buy a house with a storefront in Sungbook.

As the sun elongates my shadow, I walk home with a bag of almond cookies. I do not like to return home empty handed. From the wide, flat view that grey asphalt affords, I see my wife sitting on a stool guarding her store. She holds a fly swatter on one hand and flaps a ying-yang patterned fan with another, for flies still busily buzz about the withered food in the stalls. She is one of those creatures that bulge as they age and sweat.

Her brother's wife blames my wife, saying she made me obsolete. She is one of those who cannot accept that it is I, the man, who is blame-ridden. She and others still remember me of the old days, a star among Korea's elite artists. They remember the grand exhibition where one of my pictures, one about spring and people, won the first prize. They cannot believe it is I, the one who once shone so brilliantly, who could not, would not, cannot, or will not support a family. They say it was my wife. She was too strong. She usurped the man's role, they say.

My wife tells me such nonsense, each time something triggers her memory, or hears a comment or another. She then noisily recounts this and that injustice, blowing her nose and mopping her tears when all I try to do is to forget the day and lie still on my cot. One of the worst was the last time her sister-in-law visited to gather her share for their monthly savings association. She apparently said to my wife that I would have learned to keep a job, had I been truly forced. Who knows? Poor wife. She still nags me at times that I could teach English once I am cured. Such a thought - to huddle with young ones and repeat over and over and over the same thing - it gives me a headache. Torture, sheer torture, it would be. When she goes into such unreasonable antics, I tell her off.

"Woman, don't you know anything? Didn't I tell you that I studied art? An artist makes art!"

Cowered, she becomes mute. She does not retort, "Well then, why don't you make art?"

Well, why don't I? That is a good question. I need materials, space, and time; in short, what I have lost. Spirit. Money. I keep going over and over how it all happened. How is it that you could spend it as if there were no tomorrow and then one day you wake up and cannot find a dime? I heard that a few of my old friends are in Paris doing art. Others are dead, killed, lost, or wasted. What is art? Once in a while, when no one is looking, I do sketches of this or that on tiny papers that find their way to my room. It is true - I hanker at times, still dreaming a dream of rendering a true picture. Splashes of colors interlock, unstable, crusty, and bleeding. I lack the will.

My youngest spots me and runs towards me. She is not pretty, unlike her sister Sunmie. She has a peasant's face, big and ruddy. Her nose is flat, and her eyes, squinty. I wonder if she is my offspring. And despite all the bad food she consumes, she is chubby, round, and happy. I call her "piglet". She takes the cookies from my hand. She skips along next to me. She is happy that I have gotten up today and went out like other fathers. She is nine years old. She loves school, her village, and Korea. She belongs, blessed. My wife greets me and helps me into the inner quarters.

"Did you have a good lunch?"

"Hhm."

"And your medicine, did you take it?"

"Hhm."

She studies my face with distrust. I lie down on my cot, saying I need a rest. My oldest boy comes to greet me near dusk. My wife shuffles in after him.

"Father, I have been thinking about applying to the university. My teacher says that the Military Academy would be a good choice."

I keep quiet. Doesn't the boy know anything? Does he really want to kill and torture people? I keep quiet.

"Father?"

"Hhm. We are an old family of civilians," I finally say - to acknowledge him.

"It's very difficult to get into the Academy, Father. If I can do it, it will be free. No tuition."

Free. This child already asks so little of life. Free and he is ready to bargain his life away.

"Husband, Byungshik is correct. The world has changed. Look at President Park! And Kim Jongpil and his friends, they are all graduates of the Academy."

"We will discuss it later."

"Yes, Father."

My wife follows after her son. She quietly closes the sliding doors behind her. My wife thinks success is right. She, like others, bows before the likes of Kim Jongpil, a peasant boy turned a KCIA operative, then a prime minister. A killer. Would he say that it was the politics of the day? I must admit he looks quite honorable in recent pictures. Money makes you look honorable. Money silences the dead and the crippled.

President Park. Who ever thought a nonentity from the boondocks would become the king of new Korea? A hunting dog for the Japanese hunts the Reds under the Americans, pledging unwavering belief in the American way - two prerequisites. I appreciate the wealth of America, notions of democracy, and

America's Declaration of Independence. Only Koreans, naïve and still trusting, do not understand: "all men are created equal" does not apply to them, like it did not apply to the Negroes. How many people died putting stock in Wilson's words that all peoples shall rule themselves? Not that all is America's fault. Koreans - they played the endless games of tribal politics, refusing to see an inch in front of their noses until the Japanese swallowed Korea, and they still dance to ideologies of foreign making now that they are given their independence.

Our new masters cannot tell the difference between honorable men reduced to work for them and the rogues for the highest bidders. It is degrading to work for them when it makes no difference whether you are a toady or a man of honor, although there was that lieutenant, a fine specimen from West Point, Clifford - that was his name. He was as straight as anyone I've known and quick, capable, and friendly. I suppose Byungshik could become someone like that if he could somehow avoid being enmeshed in Park's killing machine. I will not say all this to him. I do not wish to endanger my child. Let him live and find his success, and not become like me.

I hear my second son Kwonchul coming home well after darkness has set in. He is in the last year of middle school. He has not yet mentioned if he would like to continue to high school. Lanky and sensitive, he has my spirit. His eyes are full of unrequited desires. He skips school, and even when he goes there because he has no other place to go, he passes the time sitting on the hills behind his classrooms. One of his teachers was worried enough about him to pay us a visit. I wish I had money to do him all the justice he deserves. My heart aches for him.

What is it that I, a man of forty-eight years, can do? How do I jumpstart my life? My vision fails. The disease. I will not survive this winter.

I have sired four children. I have sired them without understanding. What is this that I gave them? The sum of the years of my breathing, the cycles of nights and days come up empty, except the reckoning that it was money that had allowed my youthful flair, the mirth and congeniality of my old acquaintances, and even my old dreams of art and beauty. Money celebrates holidays; money allows summer vacations; money keeps together the family. Ask the poor when was the last time a relative came and sought his wisdom, when was the last time a stranger acknowledged his existence, when was the last time he felt at ease amidst the gazes of the petty bourgeois, and when was the last time he stood straight before anything resembling wealth? The black night thickens.

I recall it. I see, I see it. I had forgotten. A bundle in the drawer. A bundle of money. The bottom drawer. The chestnut dresser!

"Byungshik, Byungshik! Open it! Open it! The Money! Don't just stand there!" I shout to my eldest son.

"Husband, husband, wake up," someone is shaking me.

"What's wrong? Are you O.K.? Husband?"

A figure emerges. I am drenched. My wife leans over and wipes my forehead. Her hands feel soft.

"Shh, here. Here is water," she says.

Mr. Song's House

On an afternoon in late April 1972, Ayoung Jun walked up the hills to a corner store on the other side of the mountain ridge. She was already a third grader, old enough to marinate tofu for dinner as her mother instructed her the prior evening. She was passing by Mr. Song's house, a two-room structure with a kitchen on a barren lot except for one scrawny tree. The yard was large, for Mr. Song's house was the first to be built on the hills higher up than the old part of her village. Mr. Song and his family came to her part of Seoul before even more people followed them and built their houses on hills even higher up. Mr. Song's small house on the large lot reminded her of the one yellow candy still remaining in the colorful can in which it came and she could not bring herself to finish it.

Mr. Song was slowly walking, surveying his house; his two little boys trailed him, imitating him. His wife was gathering the dry laundry from the clothesline hitched from a corner of the kitchen eaves to the tree. Like most of the men in Ayoung's village, Mr. Song worked on the new roads and apartments that ushered in modernity all around the Han River, and like them, he wore a pair of black trousers and a white cotton T-shirt as the weather was fine. He was, however, unlike them in his expressions and gestures. They proclaimed some inviolable space about him. He did not look straight at people, or return their gaze, or greet any of the women who carried on their ceaseless commentaries by the crossroads of their village. He was tight and self-contained. But on that April day when Ayoung saw him, he looked happy in the full sunlight. She envied him.

A few days later, Ayoung heard from her friend Jeeyoung that Mr. Song had started to expand his house. She always knew the important news in their village before Ayoung: her father worked at the police station, and the men of the village streamed to her house, sounding him out when they were troubled or when some significant events arose in their village. Jeeyoung's house was a center of action and quite different from Ayoung's, where her mother went to work before she awoke and had not the time to mingle with others. Ayoung often knew more than her mother about their village from overhearing the women at the crossroads. Their news, however, was not as fresh or official as those from Jeeyoung's house.

"Uncle Song is going to make lots of money," said Jeeyoung. "He is building a western house, with indoor plumbing, tiled bathroom, and all, and then he is going to sell it. He is going to be the richest man in our village."

"Really?" Ayoung tried to imagine a beautiful house in her village. The first western house that she ever saw was the one across from the waterfalls, a little way up on the dirt road after crossing the metal bridge down the hills. Nestled in the hills of the opposite mountains, it was a handsome two-story redbrick, with panels of windows offering panoramic views of the waterfalls. Tall trees screened it, making it look modest, and thus more beautiful and alluring.

"I heard my father talking to the other uncles about it. It is going to be really nice!" Jeeyoung said.

"Really!" Ayoung recalled the beautiful house below. It had shiny black sedans that rolled in and out of its grey steel doors. Could a car possibly come up to her village? No. Mr. Song was not a magician. However modern his house would be, it could not be as pretty as the one across the stream either. It would be on a bare yard, a way up on bald hills where more families ever hastily propped up their makeshift dwellings.

Besides, no house could ever be as handsome, serene, and harmonious as the one by the waterfalls. It was a very special house, where even top movie stars came once and made a movie. That was long before Ayoung started school. She and her friends ran down at the heels of the older children who got wind of the news that famous movie stars were below their hills.

"Look, look! There! There is Sin Sungil! There, there is Yoon Junghee," shouted Sunhee's older sister Sunja and her friends. Ayoung and her friends, standing on their toes and holding onto the bushes behind which they hid, strained their limbs and necks to see. They could not make out the distant figures. You had to know what you were seeing to see what you were supposed to see.

No, Mr. Song's house would not be even as pretty or nice as the fancy houses that went up on the opposite mountains behind the Buddhist temple.

"I bet it won't be half as nice as the new houses across the mountains," said Ayoung.

"Of course not!" said Jeeyoung, remembering Ayoung always had a way of finding a fault. "That's not the point! Uncle Song is going to be rich! After he sells it!"

"Really?" Ayoung wondered who would pay so much money for a house in her village.

"Really, more than enough to buy another house and a lot left over, even to start a business. Houses are really expensive, and Mr. Song can make a nice house in his big yard. Except for the hills, houses here could be really, really expensive," Jeeyoung explained, getting excited over all that could be for Mr. Song. Ayoung nodded her head. Surely there were good reasons why those big houses kept cropping up on the mountain opposite them.

After her friend left for dinner, Ayoung thought about Mr. Song and his new house. He would make a house with indoor plumbing in her village, and if he succeeded, her house could have it too some day. Ayoung had been to a house with indoor plumbing. It was the house of her mother's old friend. Like her mother, Mrs. Yoo married a wrong man, and her life went all awry too. But she was not poor. She had a thriving business in Itaewon selling leather goods to the Americans and their women. Ayoung gathered this much from the exchanges between Mrs. Yoo and her mother, and watched with a strange sensation her mother comforting her friend, who was richer than Ayoung could imagine but was embarrassed about her business. Her mother told her friend she was lucky to have a thriving business, and be childless.

It was in Mrs. Yoo's house Ayoung first learned what a modern house ought to be. There were sofas and tables, and ice cubes enough to satiate anyone's thirst. Most of all, when she had to go the outhouse, all she had to do was to go inside a little room and then pulled a string. It was magic. She needed not brace herself beforehand or hold her breath; she needed not worry about a misstep; and she would not venture outdoors when it rained or was freezing.

Modern plumbing also meant the luxury of a steamy bath in one's own house. She would not broadcast to women in her village, by the way she looked and the bag she carried, how often she washed herself, even if they refrained perchance from asking where she was going. They could tell in a glance whether she was going or coming after hours of soaking and scrubbing in the bathhouse. Wonderful it would be to bathe in her very own house. Once Mr. Song had it, others would follow, and she could ask to her mother too, thought Ayoung.

On a cheery day in May, Ayoung washed her canvass shoes. She did not know when her next pair would come, and it was best not to count on things. They had a way of not coming when they were expected, like the bread she received at her school on one spring day. She was cautious at first and told herself not to expect the soft bread, which tore easily and melted deliciously in her mouth. But as it came day after day, she finally looked forward to receiving it, and it stopped just as it started: out of the blue, without an explanation. Life was like that. She had better take care of her shoes. With a dab of soap on her old toothbrush, she scrubbed away stains and dirt, and set them against the kitchen wall where the sunlight was strong; they would dry before dusk. She then started toward Mr. Song's house.

He was shoveling cement into a depression in a mound of sand, having already built a wall about three feet high around his yard. He had rolled up his trousers and was wearing a short-sleeved T-shirt, exposing his darkened arms and calves, which flexed to the rhythms of his movement. His high forehead and cheekbones glistened under the full sun. A towel around his neck sopped up his sweat.

When a gray mixture was made, Mr. Song shoveled some into a pail, added water, and stirred it with his shovel. He scooped a little onto his wooden palette, cut it several times and tossed it lightly, re-mixing the mortar. He then spread it with ease on the top of his new wall and firmly set another cinder block. He scraped oozing mortar off the wall, threw it onto his palette, re-mixed it, cutting and lobbing the lump high up. As he continued with the layering of the cinder blocks with acute concentration, his face and body moved in fine concert. His black eyes glimmered like marbles.

Mr. Song, unlike other uncles of her village, was a bundle of energy and quiet confidence. Cheering him on in her heart, Ayoung envied his two boys who followed him about. The older of the two, about five years old, was his father's assistant. He fetched tools and made sure the pail of mortar was near his father as he made his way along the wall. The other one, who darted to help when his brother yelled for him, was mostly absorbed with the mound of sand on one side of the yard. He scooped the sand at the edge back onto the pile and was pleased when the sand slid and required his further attention.

Ayoung could have kept on watching Mr. Song and his family, except for the uneasy feeling she had, which told her she was intruding. It was rude to keep on watching them, whether or not all was done in full view of any passersby. Ayoung pretended that she had a forgotten errand and picked up her pace towards the next hill. She would climb the ridge of the southern parts of the Bookak Mountains and walk along the ridge to the post of the soldiers guarding the Blue House. She would then return home, making a large circuit.

High up in the blue expanse, cotton clouds drew fantastic pictures: birds with beaks miles long, boats fading and regrouping, and strange fishes transforming to skidding faces. Closing her eyes, Ayoung counted to ten and reopened them, scanning the sky to see whether the pictures changed and whether they moved with her. Could she identify any of the faces? She could see Jesus and God the Father as Minister Jang had told her long ago. They were high up: the son looking sad and merciful, the father, stern and old with a long trailing beard.

Could she see the face of her father? He had passed away the summer of her second grade. It was a rainy day, and she was happy because she had caught a frog by the stream. Her mother stayed home, somehow knowing what the day had in store. Sighing she said to Ayoung, who came home running to show off her catch, that Father went to a world better than this one. Would he be up there? Ayoung searched. She remembered. Only Christians, only Christians would be high up in heaven.

Howsoever gentle he had been, he would not be up there. Only Christians said the minister. That was not fair, was it? What about her grandparents? If her father had chosen to disbelieve - for he had surely heard of Jesus - how about her grandparents, who may have not heard of Him? Was it fair to burn them forever and ever? If they had heard of Him and made the same choice as her father, how about her great grandparents, or great, great grandparents? Would a just God burn them in an everlasting fire? Minister Jang must have meant to add something else. Where was he? Would he have told her what happened to someone like her great, great grandparents, once he had returned home? Where was he? Closing her eyes, Ayoung prayed and resumed the walk.

By late June, Mr. Song's house was four times larger than before. A new wall closed it off on all sides except for a space between two pillars, where double gates would hang. Standing on a hill by the path that led to the corner store, Ayoung watched the nicely balanced house.

Mr. Song added two rooms and a large living room that led to the inner rooms. A door with a golden knob closed off the inner space from the yard. It was a large, modern house - and drab. The walls and the building were plastered with concrete. Their grayness disappointed her. She knew it could not be as handsome or as fancy as the redbrick houses on the opposite mountains. She had no right to be disappointed. She looked for encouraging aspects. The curved metal bars about the sliding windows were shapely. The dark brown door with the golden knob was handsome.

Besides the inside was all modern and nice, Ayoung recalled as she resumed her walk. Jeeyoung had eagerly related Mr. Song's new additions: new rooms, nice floors, a kitchen with countertops and cabinets, and especially a bathroom with small pretty tiles. As Jeeyoung described them, her animated eyes said she was as excited as Ayoung about the first western house in their village. She repeatedly said the best part was the new bathroom with shiny little square tiles. Jeeyoung too dreamed of indoor plumbing and hot water that gushed at the turn of a little faucet. Howsoever it looked, Mr. Song's house had what really counted. Not only she and Jeeyoung but also every woman in their village and others like theirs would desire such a house. Mr. Song could indeed make tons of money. Ayoung prayed he would.

On an early afternoon in July, Ayoung was helping her mother making *moolkimchi*. They brought out large radishes, hot pepper, garlic, and onions from the kitchen to the washstand. Ayoung began peeling the garlic cloves and washed them, feeling for the squeaky ivory innards, which meant she had removed their thin films. Her mother scrubbed the fat radishes hard with a rough sponge. She then rapidly sliced them. When Ayoung handed cleaned onions and garlic cloves to her, her mother handed her a slice of the radish to taste. It was crunchy, juicy, and sweet. It would make delicious *kimchi*, Ayoung was thinking, when Jeeyoung rushed through the gate calling out her name.

Ayoung ran after her friend, receiving a nod from her mother. Out of the gate, amid a crowd of women and children, they hurtled towards a vortex of screeches and bawling. They stopped before a crowd, which thronged half-circling Mr. Song's house. Ayoung stood dazed, unable to comprehend at first that the thumps, shrieks, and bawls that brought her there were the sounds of sledgehammers pounding on the house.

Dust swirled up. Each blow brought ugly gaps in the house. Two men pummeled, resolutely refusing to meet the eyes of the crowd. They pounded, relentlessly; Mrs. Song tried to block them, shuffling between the two with her limp arms.

"Stop, stop it! No!" she shrieked. "Please, somebody, somebody, please help us!"

Her two boys bawled after her. The men shoved her aside, snarling at her to move her boys. Startled, she gathered them to a corner. She then ventured to approach the men, who brushed her aside like a gnat about them. Silently they continued. Mrs. Song cried like a baby, plopping down in the middle of the yard. An old woman from the crowd helped her to move to one side. Someone gave her a cup of water, urging her to take a sip.

The small children in the crowd began to whimper. Their mothers hushed them and began taking them home. The crowd dispersed; their thick silence did not turn the whirls of dust to a dream. The men with sledgehammers departed after they completely destroyed Mr. Song's additions.

The next day, Jeeyoung related what she had heard to Ayoung. The district office had dispatched the men because Mr. Song's house was illegal.

"He did not have a permit," echoed Jeeyoung. "No one can build a house without a permit. It was not legal, and the land belongs to the government! You must have a permit to build, and it's given only if everything is proper. He did not own the land!"

Ayoung listened to her friend silently as she had listened silently to the women who were abuzz, repeating to one another what they had heard. Following a flurry of exclamations and explanations, the village turned silent. The women stopped gathering at the crossroads, as if the hot summer had turned to midwinter. Would all turn out aright, if they all stayed quiet and wished the evil away?

As with Jeeyoung's, every explanation Ayoung heard pointed out that what Mr. Song did was illegal. But that was nothing new, although she learned for the first time that the government owned all the land in her village and around it. Every house in her neighborhood and all those that cropped up higher up were then permit-less. All of them, illegal, some for years, some, generations. But who had ever cared whether a man added a room, another built up his wall, or a third plowed a garden? It was not right for the district office to send the men out and knock it down only when Mr. Song was almost done with his new house. Malicious. Everyone in her village knew that he was building his house up. The office must have known it too. Why did it wait until it was so nicely worked on, if it was to be destroyed?

Someone was envious of Mr. Song, and all the money he was going to make. Ayoung had believed the men in her village were good and decent, in the ways of Confucius, even if they were not Christians or Buddhists. You needed not be ashamed of your poverty: many good people ended up poor and worse, like Hongbu, Yi Soonshin, and the patriots who fought the Japanese. Regardless of your poverty, you could be decent. Which uncle of her village betrayed common decency? Jeeyoung's father worked at the police station. Could he have prevented the disaster? Could it be him? Kyonghee had disliked Jeeyoung, saying she was sneaky and her father, an agent. But it never sounded right to Ayoung to blame Jeeyoung's father. It was his job to support President Park; he was to police and report suspicious activities. Besides, Mr. Song was not a communist, and building one's house, not a crime.

Perhaps he did not hand out the envelopes as he was supposed to. Did he stubbornly ignore the hints and warnings? Did he worsen his luck with his undue defiance? If you wanted to rise above your station, you needed someone strong to protect you, and you had to assure those above you that you could never approach them, that whatever gain you might obtain would be miniscule, that they would always remain your superiors. It was also wise to assure your equals. Swear that your new gains were minute, that you could never, ever, forget your place. You needed to trick away the evil - the evil their envy would conjure up. Likely Mr. Song was too proud - too proud to beg, too proud to take such precautions.

Why did the two men so ferociously destroy the house? Who would have cared whether they knocked it off or razed it so completely? They were like him, working with their hands and poor. Where was their pity? Zealous, they were zealous like the guard at the mansion who had lashed at Sunhee and her. On a day in late August when they were first graders, they were playing down by the stream when they remembered the cherry tree that became enclosed in a new mansion which had gone up by the twin bridges, almost near their school. The tree was theirs before the walls had encircled it, for they climbed it and ate the cherries to their heart's content. Remembering it, they were gripped with an urge to check if its old branches had cherries again. They ran down to the house and craned to see through the gaps between the steel pickets of the gate. A wide field had been turned to a delightful garden with handsome rocks, trees, and waterfalls. She and Sunhee were pointing out different marvels to each other when the guard cracked a whip across their faces. Would his master have cared whether he lashed at the pickets and scared them away or in fact inflicted welts on them? He was fearless, certain of his power over them. Did the two men feel the same power? Or, was it shame, which intoxicated them?

About a month after the demolition, when the village seemed to settle back to its normal routines, Ayoung learned that Mr. Song was rebuilding his house. She admired the strength of his will. On a hot day in early August, she and Jeeyoung passed by his house. They were on their way to buy paper dolls at a store over the southern ridges. They had watched a long time ago, while a large crowd spilt onto the street, the television in the store, which showed - dreamlike - two men with bulbous helmets and padded suits placing an American flag on a crater of undulating dunes.

During the years that followed, the success of President Park's New Village Movement had made televisions common in such villages even as theirs, and Mrs. Keum, the owner of the T.V. house, had changed her business to renting out books and selling stationery goods, including paper princesses with arrays of beautiful dresses.

In passing by Mr. Song's house, Ayoung saw that the rubble had been cleaned and broken bricks were amassed on one side of his yard. Mr. Song was re-building the room next to the kitchen. Disheveled, he moved intensely. The muscles in his face moved in fits and starts. His pregnant wife watched him with a worried glance.

"Does he have a permit?" Ayoung asked Jeeyoung.

Jeeyoung shook her head.

"Why is he then rebuilding it?"

Jeeyoung shrugged, suggesting she did not know. She then added that he was buying new materials on credit from stores that were far away and did not know about his last house.

"What does your father say about it?"

"I don't know! I'm not your spy!" Jeeyoung shouted, sprinting forward. Ayoung bounded after her.

Mr. Song finished his second new house by mid-September. It was not as nice as his first. The two additional rooms were rebuilt, but without the golden doorknob or the large pillars for the gate. Two small, hinged windows replaced the handsome windows that Ayoung had liked. Nevertheless, Jeeyoung reported, it had indoor plumbing and a nice bathtub. Perhaps Mr. Song could still make a handsome profit; Ayoung hoped that all would work out for him, that he would pay off his debts and have some left for him and his family. You did not have to make as much profit as you first dreamed, reasoned Ayoung. Soon after, two men from the district office came and demolished the house.

Ayoung passed by Mr. Song's house one late afternoon not long after the second demolition. She was on an errand to buy some bean sprouts at the corner market for the evening meal. The store's seasonal vegetables were more expensive and were not as fresh as those in the markets down the hills, two bus stations further from her school. But bean sprouts did not grow in the garden like the spinach. As the owners of the store grew them themselves, they were as good as any in the markets below the hills. Ayoung preferred to climb first and then enjoy the downhill.

Mr. Song's house was as open as it had been on the brilliant day in the last spring. He was sitting cross-legged before a small lacquer table in the middle of his yard, drinking *soju*. His two boys, who were playing with pebbles, kept turning toward their father furtively watching him. His wife, well into her pregnancy, was by the kitchen, moving extremely slowly.

By the beginning of October, Mr. Song was rebuilding his house. The men and women of the village seemed not to notice it. No one made a comment. His third house looked shabby and terribly sad in the recent memory of his first renovation. No one came from the district office. Ayoung prayed that Mr. Song would not snap, like some did when life failed to pan out as they hoped. She prayed he would not die poor and sick. She prayed, despite the odds, he would one day find shovelfuls of money.

Goodbye, Sooni

Rumors ricocheted in Ayoung's village up on the mountains that the government planned to move the terminal for Bus Number 85 to its foothills. It would replace the wide pool below, where the mountain waters trickled in and lulled before thundering over a wide, sleek cliff. The terminal would then be miles closer to the village than its location across from Sungbook Elementary School.

The village had been changing. The families of the midwife Oh, Minister Jang, and Jeeyoung had moved out. New neighbors, whose housewives stayed within their walls rather than gather with other women by the crossroads, moved in. In addition to the radio, the households now had televisions whose antennas stuck out over the eaves and rooftops, changing the landscape and intercepting tragic dramas, comedies, national singing contests, and news, thereby swiftly introducing their viewers to new fads, ideas, and obsessions, and integrating them into the rapidly evolving national psyche. Further eroded were the old modes of entertainment: shows by traveling medicine men, shamans exorcizing evil spirits, telling and retelling of each other's stories and anecdotes, and getting together and helping each other in such labor intensive activities as making soy sauces, bean pastes, winter kimchi, and special dishes for ancestral days. The neighbors depended less on each other although a few old timers, Sunhee's mother and her old friends, continued on with their commentaries beneath the lone lamp pole of their village.

Ayoung overheard their excitement about Bus 85 on her way from school as she slowed down to greet Sunhee's mother. She never asked her how her old friend was doing although she often thought about her and wondered whether they would have continued to be good friends, had she not moved. They would have grown apart: of her old friends, Kyonghee was still around and, at times they ran into each other on their way to school, but did not stop to talk. A student at a middle school, Kyonghee was much too old to be a friend to a fourth grader and seemed embarrassed when they ran into each other. Indeed, to Ayoung, she made a strange image: an enormously heavy looking school bag slanted her body toward one side; the round collar of her school uniform made her round face look even rounder; and the mid-calf length skirt hung loosely from her as if it were independent of her. This incongruous image of Kyonghee had a way of unsettling Ayoung, in whose memory still flourished the giant of her younger days.

If Bus 85 came all the way up to the foothills, it would help students like Kyonghee, who carried school bags they could barely lift and whose schools were farther than hers, thought Ayoung. It was one thing for her to walk to school and quite another for them, even without the humidity, rain, or snow. A terminal at the foot of their hills would also be a boon to the women in her village. They shopped in the large market two bus stops below the current terminal whenever they had a large amount of shopping to do.

There in the market, you could buy all kinds of food: vegetables and fruits, fresh, dried, or pickled; grains, beans, and nuts, seasonal, dried, or powdered; fish, roe, and numerous other sea creatures, live, fresh, salted, dried, or pickled; different shades of green seaweed, fresh, dried, fried, or roasted; and all kinds of rice cakes, white, green, pink, pockmarked with beans, coated with yellow bean powders, stuffed with honey, scented with herbs, or stamped with lotus flowers or rhombuses. And the butchers there knew how to cut just the right part for the special meal you had in mind, or to recommend just the right kind for the budget you had. There were also shops for regular clothes;

specialty shops for coats, uniforms, underwear, *hanbok*, hats, and shoes; stores for pots and pans and all kinds of tools and accessories; and variety stores that sold fabrics, yarn, buttons, beads, zippers, and whatnots, which some women in her village knew how turn into beautiful clothes.

Ayoung's own mother shopped there when she had enough money to fill bags of groceries. She then walked home like the other women of the village, stopping often to catch her breadth, especially after crossing the metal bridge where the hills began to rise sharply. She wouldn't pay for the fare when the bus ride was shorter than the distance she had to walk from the terminal to the foothills. However, if it moved to where the mountain waters gathered, she and other women of the village might be induced to take the bus.

However, it would make no difference to her, thought Ayoung. Taking a bus was an adult affair, or for older students like Kyonghee. Whoever heard of an elementary school student riding a bus to school? It wasn't that far from her house, and riding it, expensive. Once in a while, a few students came to her school riding shiny, dust-free, black cars, but to Ayoung, they were different species from her. Indeed, after attending her school for a few days or a week, like lost birds finding their way, they inevitably left for private schools, where they would wear smart uniforms and their mothers believed they would learn to score high on college entrance examinations. They were the rich kids.

The road project was finished by the end of the summer of 1973. The stream, parts of which had been wider than twice Ayoung's height, disappeared, as did the one lane dirt road. Grey asphalt supplanted the pebbles, rocks, and beaches, as well as the lichens and moss that waxed and waned on the rocks in the stream depending on the water level. A wide, gently sloping road replaced them all, even the wide cliff that had looked so high to her. An idling bus at the brand new terminal replaced the lapping, plopping, buzzing noises of the mountain waters.

The thin metal bridge, which used to freeze and scared Ayoung and her friends when it snowed, disappeared; with it, the soft layers of white fluff all along the edges of its circular holes. She would no longer walk over the southern ridges of the mountains to bypass it when it snowed heavily or be afraid of slipping or getting her feet caught in its holes. The fear of the bridge was no more. She too benefited from the progress.

The progress which she had heard so often and was taught to memorize - the amounts of annual increase in Korea's steel production and the increases in its exports - was no longer only hearsay. She was partaking in its leaps and bounds toward modernity. She was proud. Her village too was becoming a part of the wealth and luxury she conjured up when she imagined the West.

As she walked to and from school, Ayoung began to learn the realities of the new asphalt. No white or yellow lines neatly defined the grey surface. No bushes, flowers, or shiny cars changed the view of it. The sky must have been the same as it had been but seemed lower as it hovered over grey uniformity. People, too, looked smaller on that wide surface. Like her, they had learned to turn from the street when they heard the rumble of a bus coming near and waited until the dirt it whipped up and its fume dispersed sufficiently.

If she closed her eyes, she could see the stream, pebbles, white eddies bouncing around the rocks, and the foam by the waterfalls. A man whose name no one knew had lived in a hut near the cliffs. He had bushy hair in which seemed to grow white flowers. Her heart jumped with fear when she first saw him, but in time she grew to look for him by the stream and imagined stories about him.

He was a soldier who had run away during the war. Was he a communist who survived hiding, or a patriot who had lost his family? Perhaps he had come to Seoul to make a fortune and was too ashamed to return home. Did his wife curse her fate and run away, or was she praying for his return home with her palms pressed together before a bowl of clear water morning and evening? Maybe he had had a reversal of fortune, like her father and many others whose stories were layered in her memory. He was gentle. Her father said once that the strange man by the waterfalls had been a scholar. She missed the uncle on whose head grew white flowers. She even missed the metal bridge with doughnut-sized holes.

Sooni Choi was a new fourth grader at Sungbook Elementary School. During a talent show at the beginning of the school year, she sang. She sang beautifully like Miss Yi Mija, the Maria Callas of Korean pop music. Her voice would rise and rise, high, high up, and would subside and flutter to sad lyrics of a love song. Everyone who heard Sooni marveled at her singing. The teachers began to borrow her for their music classes, and she came to Ayoung's class too and pealed out sorrowful songs about lost daughters, lost lovers, and lost homeland. Her voice rang clearer than the clearest bell Ayoung ever heard. Sooni had talent.

She lived a good twenty-minute hike up from Ayoung's house. They became best friends, for no other girls in their grade lived up on the hills of their village. They walked home together, and sometimes Ayoung walked all the way to Sooni's house and stayed there until early evening. She did not like the emptiness in her house, where her mother came home late from work and left early in the morning before she woke.

Sooni's house was one room with an outdoor kitchen on a newly flattened hill. She and her parents moved from Cholla Province because Seoul was where work was. Like a giant magnet, it pulled in every family that could up and move. Sooni's house was smaller and dimmer than Ayoung's, but it was less dreary than hers, for Sooni's mother was always home: cooking, cleaning, sewing, or occupied with other chores. The one piece of furniture in the room was a dresser. On the top of it were folded blankets, which they used to sleep on at night.

One day in November, Ayoung's mother gave her a box of crayons. Opening the brightly colored box, she saw the four rows of beautiful colors. She thought she could make all the colors in the world with them. Her mother was sure to buy only the best for her when she could. She bought a most luxurious fur coat for her when she was a first grader although it was the only warm coat she had for several years, until the sleeves became too short and the fur became mangy.

She showed her crayons to Sooni the next day. She was as excited about them as Ayoung. They began a game of drawing and coloring pictures. They drew princesses in their beautiful dresses, beautiful houses with windows and flowers, fields of trees, rivers, and mountains. Most of all, they drew big yellow suns. They used the crayons together, but when Ayoung left Sooni's house, she gathered and took them home with her. Once in a while, she thought she saw envy in Sooni's eyes.

Should she leave them for Sooni, wondered Ayoung. It would be nice to do so. Good people like Confucius and Jesus would have done so. Ayoung hesitated and then argued against it. They were hers. It was a fact, like the fact that Sooni had a talent. Why would Sooni be envious of her crayons when she could never sing like her? No matter how hard she tried, she would not come close to Sooni's singing and she would be crazy to envy Sooni's talent. Likewise, Sooni had no reason to envy her, thought Ayoung. The crayons were hers. She was right to take them with her. Still, was it better to leave them behind?

One afternoon in December, when they were coloring their pictures, Sooni said, "I have the same crayons, too."

"Really? The same?" Ayoung was happy to hear it. They could color so many more pictures, she thought. Her set was getting old. She waited for Sooni to bring hers out. But she did not move to show Ayoung her new crayons. Instead, she just continued with her picture.

Why was she not bringing them out, wondered Ayoung. If she had crayons as good as hers, why not show them? Could she really have the same forty-eight brilliant colors? Sooni was concentrating on her picture.

"Do you really have the same set?" Ayoung asked.

Sooni nodded, without taking her eyes off the picture.

"Do you really have them?"

"Yes!"

"Where are they?" Ayoung looked around the small room that did not show a trace of the brilliant box.

"You really have them?" she persisted.

Blushing, Sooni returned Ayoung's gaze with a look of defiance. She then turned her head toward her mother, who was quietly darning a sock by the door. She was always darning, or doing something when she was inside the room. Without meeting Sooni's gaze, her mother just continued on with her work. Sooni too went back to her drawing. The newness of Ayoung's crayons had long disappeared. Many of their favorite colors were only stumps.

"Do you really have the same set?" Ayoung asked again.

Sooni stopped coloring, pursed her lips, got up, and slid open the top drawer of the dresser. She took out some soft linen; unwrapping them, she showed a crayon box. It was the same bright box as Ayoung's had been, and in it, the forty-eight brilliant colors. Ayoung noticed a few had been very slightly used. Dumbfounded, she gazed at Sooni and then her mother. Sooni's mother could explain her confusion even if Sooni could not! Mrs. Choi did not answer her gaze.

She and Sooni were great friends. It was only natural they shared her crayons. Ayoung had thought Sooni also would have done the same. But the way Sooni's had been kept, wrapped like jewels and placed in the top drawer, told Ayoung - she was never meant to use those crayons. Sooni's mother must have had a hand in it, but she just sat quietly by the door, refusing to dispel Ayoung's confusion and embarrassment. She hurriedly finished her picture and ran down the hills from Sooni's house.

It was just like her mother said, Ayoung thought. These people in their village were ignorant, cheap, and base. She disliked her mother when she said such things. The women of her village were kind, and it was not their fault if they were uneducated, she had always thought. But she could now see her mother was right: she was sure Sooni's mother never went to school, unlike her mother.

Her own family came to live on the hills of Sungbook only because they had a bad turn of fortune. She did not know what had caused the fall, but she had heard many a time that her family would have been rich, but for a stock market crash, which drove many to suicide and ruin.

Her family was not at all like these country yokels who were filling up the hills above her house. She would never visit Sooni again, Ayoung told herself.

When the following spring came, the women in her village were abuzz again. The government had declared that the mountains in Seoul needed to be restored. It declared the hills of their village and the hills higher up, where new shanties had been cropping up, as Seoul's new green belt. The houses were to be razed and trees replanted. The women were exceptionally excited because no one knew which houses were included in the first phase that was to occur that spring. Conflicting rumors swirled, each asserting their veracity on the authority of the district office, which did not confirm the boundary for the first phase until the Friday before the evacuation date.

Ayoung was all ears to catch the buzzing voices of the adults in her village. She learned that her house and other houses in the old parts of the village were spared from the first phase. She mulled that it was probably because they had been there for a long time, before the war, and perhaps even before the Japanese rule. Poet Han Yongwoon, a national treasure and a leader in the March First Movement, had lived in the village. She could recite bits of his famous songs, songs about lost Korea.

> My love is gone. O my beloved is gone.
> Breaking blue lights of the mountains,
> Towards red maple groves, I walked . . .
> The memories of our razor-sharp first kisses . . .
> Turned the needle of my destiny and disappeared . . .

It was a sad song - piercing, beautiful. Yet, his songs were less sad than those of Kim Sowol. They lived at a time when their world was turning topsy-turvy, when the revered became simply old, useless. How did they ever learn to wear suits and cut off their topknots? At least she did not live under the Japanese rule, or run for a shelter during a bombardment. And she needed not move; telling so, Ayoung allayed herself.

Her world was the village. She could not imagine living anywhere else. How would she feel if she had to move? Could the government really pick her up and move her to a place she did not know and never imagined for herself? What about her feelings? Her affections and love for the familiar houses, faces, streets, and the hills? They were in her, inseparable from her. How could the government ever compensate for them? Could she protest and sit in the middle of her yard until her face turned blue? Could she throw rocks at the officials and curse at them? Perhaps. Unlikely. She would be removed if she were so designated. Whether dragged, hoisted, beaten up, or taken to re-education, or whether she submitted without a peep, she would be gone. She might even try to curry favor with the officers, in fear, in a wish to please, and in shame. Being friendly was nothing bad, she would justify. Being friendly with those above her could even help her, couldn't it? she would justify. In the end, she would be removed.

On the opposite mountains, across what had been the stream, two story houses with large windows and verandas had sprouted as the shanties cropped up on her side. If the government wanted to keep the mountains green, why did it let those big houses be built? Why did it blast and shave the mountains for tunnels and roads? None of the uncles, aunts, or children of her village rode the shiny black sedans that whizzed through the tunnels and glided on the mountain roads before stopping at the gray steel doors of those houses. They were huge, any of them, three, five times larger than a house in her village. Why did the government let those houses be built up on the opposite side? Only a few years ago, they were forests, except for the Buddhist temple and the one most exquisite house across from the waterfalls.

Sooni's house was in the area that the government declared should be demolished that spring. Ayoung wished to go and visit her. Many times before the evacuation, she walked out of her gate and started toward Sooni's house. She then stopped. She had not visited it for months. She had not often seen Sooni, for the teachers had stopped asking her to sing a long while ago: the novelty of seeing a young girl trilling heartaches like Yi Mija had worn out, and likely, a parent raised objections. Some people looked down on those songs Sooni sang: they were too Korean, too old fashioned, and too popular with the ignorant, with the poor, they said. Sooni also had a new friend, a girl who had moved to a house near hers.

After trudging up the first hill toward Sooni's house with great eagerness, Ayoung inevitably turned her steps back toward her home. She told herself they did not have the time to renew their friendship. In her farewells, she would be clumsy and exaggerate their friendship. She would be false, thought Ayoung.

On the day of the evacuation, a few women of her neighborhood were going to say goodbye to the people being removed. Small children ran alongside their mothers. An old neighbor, who saw Ayoung standing amid the flow of the people, gestured toward her to come with her. It would be easy, easy to tag along, Ayoung saw, but told herself that it was too late. Too late to say a proper goodbye among the clamoring people, between the hollers, shouts, and exchanges of well-meaning, futile wishes. No. She would not go. She would not witness people with pots and pans on their head, and babies and bundles on their back being rounded up. She would not watch the officials hustling to haul them from one corner of Seoul to another. No. She would not witness Sooni's shame and humiliation - or were they hers?

On the steppingstone that led to the kitchen of her house, Ayoung sat and waited. She waited for the noise of the women coming back and the sounds their children made. She leaped to her feet. Their voices were approaching the edges of her neighborhood. She bolted. Up on the edges of the cliffs, below which had been a pool of the mountain water, she saw heads peeping out of the windows of an idling bus. Ayoung focused all of her senses to identify the faces. The bus began to belch and rumble down the asphalt, leaving a wake of black fumes. The number 85 in large black in a thick red circle fitfully showed through dusty grayness, turning smaller and smaller.

She was sorry. She was sorry for her smallness. She heard Sooni pealing love-songs.

Miran

Miran met Minkyu when she was a junior in high school. She was looking for an English exercise book when she noticed a boy stealing glances at her. She had seen him several times in the same bookstore, a three-story building, each floor crammed with shelves and stalls and all of them overflowing with books. It attracted all kinds of students and booklovers.

The boy had unusually white skin and a shyness about him. She smiled at him. She was to ignore any such attention and respond only with indifference. Miran, like most girls of her age, did not violate school codes or social decorum that forbade them from dating, wearing skirts that came higher than their ankles, or letting their long hair loose. And she was not one of those reputed to be wild and have boyfriends, those about whom their classmates' incessantly gossiped, disdained, envied, and censured. But the boy seemed so shy and timid; it seemed harmless to give him a smile.

Miran placed the books she was browsing back on the shelves. She would first see if she could borrow them from her friends. As she walked out of the store, Minkyu followed her. She increased her pace, regretting her smile. His boldness surprised her, as did the sense of thrill she felt. She trotted fast and overshot the bus stop where she would normally take Bus 85. She would walk to the next stop, by then, she hoped, he would have taken his own bus. Instead Minkyu closed in right next to her.

"Why do you walk so fast? Slow down!"

She ignored him, trying to steady her dizzying head.

"What kind of a girl are you to walk so fast? See, I am out of breath," he said, grinning.

Miran increased her pace.

"I mean no harm, slow down a little."

"Why are you following? Is this your habit?"

"No, never! Slow down some, will you? How can I answer you, with you moving so fast?"

Miran slowed down and turned toward Minkyu. He smiled at her brightly. He wasn't so shy after all. She liked him better for that.

Minkyu started to wait for Miran by the bus stop near the bookstore and walked her along her bus route, past the wide avenue by Seoul National University, past Changkyong Palace, and to Haehwa Rotary Circle, where he took Bus 105 towards his house near Namsan Mountain, and Miran took Bus 85 to Sungbook. She lived with her mother and her younger brother Chul in a village on the top of one of its hills. In about three years, Minkyu was in college and Miran began her first job.

"Are you going to the festival?" Miran asked Minkyu as they shared a plate of steamed dumplings after her shift at the department store. It was the beginning of September 1971, and the first college festival for Minkyu and his classmates were only two weeks away. Miran was anxious, even though she kept telling herself to be confident and generous with him. Surely he deserved it, and she shouldn't stand in the way if he wished to mingle with his college friends.

"Hhm," he answered without taking his eyes off the dumpling he was gripping with his chopsticks.

"You haven't asked me if I would go with you."

Minkyu opened his small eyes wide and watched her as if it never crossed his mind. He then broke into a broad smile and ruffled his hair, which he had grown out since his graduation.

"I didn't know you wanted to mingle, you know, with those snotty students. I thought you didn't like them," he said. Minkyu

109

had vague ideas for the festival. He could bond with his classmates and perhaps get to know some of the pretty girls. But also, he was not sure if he wanted to go. It was not one of those famous festivals at top universities. His test scores were not good enough for them, and when he failed to get into one of them, his mother became ill and was bed ridden for months. Of course he did not give a damn about those schools, but he was not sure if he wanted to participate in a second rate festival. He had thought also that he should minimize his college activities, for Miran. He did not wish to drag her into events and people, of which she was not a part. Why make her feel insecure or awkward about not attending college? She was doing more than most girls: she was helping out her family.

"Why, did you want to go?" Minkyu asked Miran, reassessing his assumptions.

"No, I was just curious. I wondered what your plan was," she said, picking up a glass of water.

Minkyu had learned to read her gestures. When she hid her face while she answered, it meant she was answering a half-truth, something other than what she truly wanted. Such acts of Miran nettled him at first, for he wished her to be honest with herself and trust him. But he had learned too that such a demand was often asking too much of her.

"If you like, we will go together," he said, reaching for another dumpling. He would be the talk of the festival if he showed up with a girlfriend of three years. Most of the boys, he would bet, did not even know how to talk to a girl.

"You think, really?" Miran gave him one of her sweetest smiles. She had not applied to college, but had not extinguished her desire to experience college life.

Miran Paek was triumphant at the festival. She captivated Min-kyu's classmates, for she was charming with her long flowing hair, a winning smile, and a slender body which she knew how to move sensuously to the sounds of acoustic guitars, bugles, and gongs. She was a graduate of a high school for arts, and her specialty was traditional Korean dancing. If a few females in their circle objected to this new girl among them, they muted their displeasure, for they were young and still too innocent to ridicule their own sex in public, especially before her captivated male admirers. Also, none of them guessed she was a mere sales clerk. Miran confirmed to herself that she was as pretty, in fact prettier than most of the girls in Minkyu's class and that she and Minkyu had a connection, which these girls could not easily disturb. She really needed to stop fretting about his college life. He was hers, she, his.

In mid-October, while they walked beneath the high stone-walls of the palace as they had done day after day during their high school years, Miran approached the subject of introducing Minkyu to her mother.

"My mother is asking me if I was dating. I told her about you," Miran said.

"Hhm."

"You could come and visit us one of these weekends."

"Hhm."

"Why, don't you want to?"

"I do, of course. It's just so sudden. You know, we had not discussed it, not seriously anyway. I will come, of course, uh, after the New Year. Things are getting really hectic, you know, the exams, the end of the year activities, you know, family obligations and visits."

Minkyu loved her and would do anything for her, he felt, although he could not exactly pinpoint what made her so tender to

111

him: a dimple on her left cheek when she smiled, her delicate frame, her family that was very different from his, or the strange mixture of shyness and street smartness that ached his heart. He was also a romantic. He dreamed of one consuming love for himself, the kind the poets wrote about. His life would not be worth much and he would feel cheated, he thought, if he did not experience the high passion of one true love, despite the fact that he quietly acquiesced when his peers talked of love casually and offhandedly. But what kind of woman was Miran's mother? She must have known that Miran had been dating him. What mother would be so lax with her daughter? And what kind of girl was Miran? He had naturally paid for their snacks and movies together; gradually, he had even helped her with her school expenses, and he certainly had not minded sharing his pocket money with her or using the money for his after-school-lessons on her. He had overruled her protests, saying she would have done the same had their situation been reversed. He was willing. But what mother could be so permissive? What kind of woman was . she?

Minkyu came and visited Miran's family in March. He then came often, saying he liked her mother's cooking and being close to God up in the mountains. He could not believe he was still in Seoul when he first visited her house. He walked about two miles on a one-lane dirt road after getting off at the last stop. The road switched its side a few times with a wide stream. In it, water tumbled over rocks and boulders, betraying the continual, upward slope he and Miran were making from the terminal to the hills of her village. After crossing a thin metal bridge patterned with circular holes, they climbed veritable hills on a meandering path. Every inch of the land was in use, a house, a garden, or a dump.

He had never been in such close contact with the immediacy of human needs or struggles for survival. And despite the rawness and ugliness that surrounded Miran's house, it felt in many ways authentic and even wholesome to Minkyu, certainly more so than his house, where all of his needs were easily met, or were assumed to be.

Miran's mother and her neighbors complained, gossiped, and laughed loudly in the open, sharing old fashioned rice cakes he had never seen or tasted before. At her house, he saw squawking chickens for the first time and retrieved toasty eggs from their coop. He learned to milk a goat and helped Miran's mother in bottling the milk. She delivered warm milk to a few households in the village. In addition to selling what the chickens and the goat produced, Mrs. Paek sold marinated and pickled dishes to the merchants in the market two stops before the terminal. She also hired herself out as a day-hand when the houses below the hills needed extra help. She was renowned for her cooking and her colorful personality. When she drank, an occasional occurrence, she would loudly recall all those who had crossed her and cursed them roundly.

The wonder was that she managed to educate her two children even though Miran's high school was cheaper than it would have been because it was a heavily subsidized school for arts. Only those talented in music, art, or dancing could attend it, and Miran had a knack for Korean dancing. Chul, her younger brother, was a junior in high school. He was brilliant, if stiff-necked and gloomy. Despite a mother who worshipped the ground he walked on, he often triggered in her endless pleas and complaints. Howsoever solicitous Mrs. Paek was of Minkyu's good opinions, she also did not attempt to hide her feelings and flaws in her family. Such intimacy seemed to him real honor and friendship.

Following one of Minkyu's visits in July when sweet fragrances of the early summer had faded and the summer was reaching its lush vigor, Chul cornered Miran.

"You have to think about your relationship with Minkyu. He does not respect us, not you, not Mother, none of us."

"What did he do? What's wrong?" Miran had dreaded something like this. "He is nice to us. He is smart, and generous."

"Generous! With all his money, why wouldn't he be? He can take it somewhere else. The point is he does not respect us. I don't want him coming here."

"I thought you liked him. What is the matter?" Miran tried to figure out what had gone wrong that evening; she could not remember anything particular. She had been anxious when Minkyu first came to visit them, for Chul was keenly sensitive, adamant about his opinions, and highly intelligent. But he seemed friendly enough to Minkyu, and Miran had been relieved.

"I have tried to deny it. I have looked the other way. I cannot stand it! How you could have met him in high school? How could Mother have let you? You don't deny it, do you?"

Miran stood silently. She was apologetic and understood what was ailing Chul. Bits of information that Minkyu had let slip - he did not have as much to fear as she - must have come together and formed a conviction in Chul.

"How could you? How could our mother?"

That she met Minkyu in high school was fatal, or could be fatal, but she was not such a girl. The implications Chul was making, or anyone else other than her mother would make, did not apply to her. Miran defended herself after a long silence.

"We are not in high school. We didn't do anything shameful. I did not mean to hurt you. You know I am not the kind you make me to be. You must trust me."

"It's not just the matter of when it started. You know it too. He should not be coming here so often. He wouldn't have, if he respects you and gave it a bit of thought. Have you met his parents? His family?"

"He is still in college!" Her voice sounded more shrilled than it ought to have been, and Miran winced. Indeed, she had noticed with somewhat troubled feelings, which she brushed aside, how easy Minkyu was becoming with her mother. She was also put out when he asked her a few days ago whether something like "Love Story" could happen in Korea. She laughed it away, saying that he was no Ryan O'Neal. However, his question did raise doubts about their relationship and how he thought of it. She had allayed her fear, repeating to herself that she would be all right, no matter what happened.

"He is nice to me, always sweet and gentle. Who knows how it will pan out? No one put iron clasps on us, I mean, no one knows the future. What I can say is I did not mean to hurt you. I will be all right, I promise. And you know, mother and I, we would never do anything to hurt you, or anything to make you ashamed of us. You know that, don't you?" She waited for Chul's response as the last sunrays dimmed. Half turned from her, he did not reply. She turned to walk toward the house.

"He is not going to marry you!" Chul shouted after her, unable to control his passion and his disappointment on hearing her steps. The night was falling fast. Miran paused briefly but continued on with her steps.

Chul Paek wished he had not broached the subject. He should have said something nice to her. She had wished to hear a few of words of encouragement, or failing that, a few words of conciliation. He was a coward and a hypocrite. Always receiving, he knew not how to give. Whatever benefits his sister had received from Minkyu, they flowed to him too. Concerns for his welfare played a part, he was certain, in his mother's decision to turn a blind eye to Miran dating in high school. His mother would do anything for him; he hated it. His sister now was telling him she would the same! If he could only disappear! He would if he had the guts!

Miran could swear she was not thinking of love when she first smiled at Minkyu. She was not thinking of love as they started to walk together along the walls of the Palace or even when he began to help her with school expenses. He was there for her when she began to look for him. When was that? She could not pinpoint it.

Old-fashioned and insistent in his ways, her brother was often at odds with people and reality about him. She admired him precisely for such qualities. But they also made him look foolish and strange. He was not the one to give advice on relationships. What he knew he read from books, and his way was to discard all things that disturbed his peace. It was not yet the time to be introduced to Minkyu's family. There was the college and the military service. She and Minkyu needed to think carefully before they approached his family. Not because she wasn't as good as anyone, of course she was, but there were issues: her lack of a college education, and her family.

A few weeks later, when the rainy season was passing, Minkyu brought up the subject of introducing Miran to his mother. They were walking towards her house after getting off at the terminal. Daytime merchants had gathered up their wares, but as the evening was still young, the merchants of the evening were only beginning to prepare mobile carts for such snacks as hot spicy rice gnocchi, fish ball soup, and leek pancakes. The curls of the smoke and the smell from their gas cookery sent out inviting lures; the bald light bulb dangling beneath their umbrellas hastened the retreat of the remaining light.

"You wanted us to wait didn't you?" said Miran, thinking he must have picked up on Chul's changed attitude. He was acting surly and bitter since the time he reproached her. And Minkyu was susceptible.

"I have been visiting your family more than a half of year, you know. It would look better if we were official, won't it?"

"My mother is at it again. She now insists that her friend's daughter is the perfect match for me. I really don't think I should go through it, and she won't take my 'No' for an answer," he added between pauses.

"Who is she? Have you seen her?"

"A few times, I believe. We were in middle school. Truthfully I don't remember her. It was long ago. I really don't know why she is showing up. Of course, it is my mother's idea," said Minkyu facing only the front of him, as Miran watched his white profile. It seemed to be receiving all the light of the early dusk and those spilling from the mobile carts. He was dear to her. Once he met this girl, things could snowball between the families, couldn't it? He was not like Chul, not as willful or as stubborn.

"What if your mother objects to me? I thought we would plan, have some plans in case," Miran stuttered.

"I understand. As it is, we will first see how it goes. Wouldn't it be better, really superb, if we got engaged? Who knows, you could even study then."

Generous and optimistic, Minkyu could build a castle in the air. At least he did not shrug or say, "I don't know," thought Miran. He could not assure her, she knew. It was wrong for her to seek it when his parents had not met her. How could he imagine the insecurity she felt regarding his family? But he should!

117

He must know! Miran's inside began to boil. Did he not care about their future? Was Chul right? He should have told her about his family's pressure on him. She could then have thought of something. They could have appeased his mother and earned some more time. But how would more time be helpful? Her family, her situation was not likely to change.

"When does your mother want to see me?" she asked, reminding her to be hopeful. No one knew the future.

"She is eager to meet you. I proposed the day before we part for the beach." Miran's heart leaped with fear.

"You did not tell her about our trip, did you?"

"Of course not. You worry too much. I told her I was going for the weekend with two guys from the university. She was happy to hear that. She did not think I was making a good use of my college years. Don't worry about her. She is very modern. You'll see."

The breeze of the previous week was a false start. Summer raged back, forcing people to acknowledge it was still supreme, regardless of their wishes for its antics to end. Feeling the sweat moistening her neck, the creases of her elbows, and the backs of her knees as she walked down the hills of her village, Miran thought that she must have gone mad. Appear modest she must, but she needed not have chosen a long sleeved white blouse and a calf-length blue skirt, as if she were still in high school.

Apprehension and insecurity seemed to have turned her into a child, timid, needy, and greedy. Was she reaching beyond her reach, knowing full well she would fail? She could not have abandoned the path she was on, not merely because she was now reaching and had been doing so the last three, four years, but also because she had hope. If they would look only at her, she would not be found amiss. His mother, his father, or his grand-

118

mother would see the pearl in her if they would only take the time to see it. It would have been better if someone else accompanied his mother; if there were two, or three persons, she was sure, at least one of them would see her true worth.

Miran entered a discreet café near Minkyu's university, away from the main stretch studded with shops, bakeries, cafes, bistros, beauty salons, and bookstores. She and Minkyu had spent many hours in it, talking of their dreams and fantasies in the atmosphere filled with French things and chansons. Minkyu was watching the entrance and waved to her as she entered it. He was wearing the blue Oxford shirt she bought for him. Sitting across from him was a slender woman, who must be in her fifties but looked more like his older sister.

Greeting her, Miran bowed politely. His mother returned her greetings with a pleasant voice, that round, mellow feminine voice without an edge. Sitting down on a chair Minkyu pulled for her, across from his mother and next to him, Miran felt relieved. Mrs. Kim effused soft elegance as she waited quietly for the waitress in black to appear. She gently acknowledged the server as she carefully placed a cup of coffee before each of them. Perhaps Minkyu was right; perhaps she was not a difficult person.

"Minkyu says that you are not in college. You must be envious of the college kids. I would be. I could not have imagined not going to school at your age, and you are so pretty," Mrs. Kim said, without touching her coffee.

"Yes, it's easy to think that way. I understand it. But one learns in so many different ways, and I do at my job. I also learn a lot from Minkyu. He shares with me what is reading, and I try

119

to do my part and learn on my own. Besides, one cannot always have everything one wants," Miran answered honestly as she thought.

"That is true," Mrs. Kim said, watching her son with a slight smile. "Life is about compromises. Isn't it Miran, may I call you Miran? Addressing you as Miss Paek would sound awkward, as if we were in an office or a store."

Miran nodded, blushing. Did she know that she was a sales clerk? Confused, Miran watched the creamy brown surface of the coffee in her cup. The lady continued.

"Accepting that you cannot have everything you want in life, now that takes some intelligence. I bet such a thought never entered Minkyu's mind. He is the only son. He does not think about compromises. I wonder what you can learn from him. He is so naïve. So, you work at Mimi's Department Store?"

Miran nodded and hoped that her face would not show the heat she was feeling despite herself. She sat up and returned the lady's gaze.

"It's strange that I did not see you before. I used to shop there until Sinrim opened recently. I suppose lots of pretty girls work there. How funny, we could have met many a time," continued Mrs. Kim.

Slowly stirring his coffee, Minkyu was quiet as if he were fishing for some precious catch and it took all his concentration. Why was he not helping her? thought Miran. They were in this together. Did he not notice where his mother was going? Couldn't he at least change the subject? Miran looked at him. Minkyu was continuing with stirring. His mother had a bemused look on her.

"I heard Sinrim is a beautiful store. I haven't been there; I didn't have an occasion. But, if you come to Mimi's, please stop by at the jewelry section. I promise, you will receive the best service," said Miran, with a regret and a slight smile.

"Thank you. It's unlikely. I hardly shop for jewelry these days, and when I do, I go to the specialty shops. These days there are so many beautiful fakes, one can trust only the very best jewelers," said Minkyu's mother, smiling inwardly at Miran.

She was charming, Mrs. Kim could see. It was not that she could not be sympathetic. Of course, she was. Who in this country did not know about poverty? But why should her own son choose a girl who could not afford university, not even a two-year college? Many girls were as pretty as she and better educated. They could offer him connections and wealth. They were indispensable in this country, no matter what starry-eyed young ones might say. Of course no one would say it so bluntly, so coarsely. But theirs was such a world.

"Well, I am not sure if Minkyu mentioned it to you, but we are to meet his father for lunch. Please excuse us," she stated politely and firmly to Miran.

"Mother!" Minkyu finally seemed to find his voice. "We were going to have lunch together, Mother! Wasn't that the plan?" He growled as his mother was getting up.

"Was it? I must have forgotten to tell you. Father wanted to meet us this afternoon. You know how busy he is. I could not possibly say no to him. I am sure Miran understands it, don't you?"

"Miran, come with us, you should come with us. Please?" begged Minkyu, turning from his mother. She was already in the middle of the café.

The meeting could not end this way. Perhaps his father would help him, even though he always demanded more from him than his mother. Miran gazed at him, shutting down the tears that welled in her.

"Don't worry about me. Please, have a nice lunch," she said, taking a sip of coffee to look nonchalant.

"Miran, I am really sorry about this. I will get back to you as soon as I can, I promise." Minkyu hastened after his mother who was nearing the door.

"I am really sorry, Miran," Minkyu repeated when he called her at work.

"I am alright, really! We'll meet as we planned. Make sure you don't forget any thing important," she answered lightly. She had decided not to change her plans on account of his mother.

She had expected objections from Minkyu's family, but did not believe in they would have the final say. She was beautiful and talented. She was good and generous. She believed in these qualities and could not imagine, even after the meeting, they would be of no consequence. All the stories she had heard and believed, the good triumphing their adversity, could not be false. They could not be lies, and she would not let Mrs. Kim turn her world upside down. It would not be so easy as she seemed to figure. By the old times' standards, she was already impure. She would not play the game of splitting her mind and body. If she were to get hurt, she would get hurt deeply. She would let him go, if she must - on her own terms.

In late November, when it was so cold that her cheeks burned, Miran called Minkyu's mother. She had a vague notion that she must see her. Their last encounter had the effect of crystallizing Miran's vague fear into a tangible opposition in the form of Mrs. Kim. Faced with it, Miran knew only to strengthen her love for Minkyu, rendering him more precious to her. And while she told

122

herself not to dwell on the future, she harbored the hope they would find a way.

"Ah, here you are," Minkyu's mother said as she sat down at the table in a café near Miran's department store. Her tone was icier than the weather outside.

"Thank you for coming," Miran bowed.

"Not at all. I was thinking we needed to meet without Minkyu present," said Mrs. Kim.

"If you would give me a chance," Miran was saying, when Mrs. Kim cut her off.

"The reason I wanted to see you is not because I have changed my mind. I know you two have been seeing each other. His father and I, we will never accept you. It will be the best if you stopped here."

"Mother,"

"How dare you to address me that way? Listen carefully. I am fully aware of your situation. Do not force me to come and create a scene at your house. Ask anybody. What kind of girl tricks an innocent boy in high school? What mother would allow it? Ask anybody. From what I hear, your brother is about to enter university. It all depends on you. Stay away from my Minkyu."

Mrs. Kim then took out an envelope from her Chanel bag and put it in front of Miran.

"Listen! This is the last time I am seeing you. You cannot possibly wish for anything else. Think of your brother; the shame you will cause him. I may not be what you wished for as Minkyu's mother, but I am frank in my own ways. You will find a generous sum."

"I did not ask for money!"

"There can be nothing else."

123

Miran walked toward a bus stop. She then changed her direction, away from the buses and cars, and trudged up the old, meandering paths that she knew from her childhood. She would eventually run into the southern hills of the Bookak Mountains and reach her house in a long, roundabout way. She did not wish to run into any acquaintances, or Minkyu. He might be looking for her. Her brain burned. She craved to cut through the feeling of strangulation. Why did she pick up the envelope? What should she do with it? She ran after Minkyu's mother when she returned to her senses. Mrs. Kim was being driven off, having had her chauffer wait outside the café.

She had believed in fairytales. Despite the nonchalant attitude she sometimes took up about love and marriage, she believed in one true love. While absurd and irrational, her first smile at Minkyu had sealed him as her love. Her casualness toward him, it must have been her own confidence. She deserved the happiness that belonged to a beautiful girl. She believed in her happiness.

Mrs. Kim was right. She could use the money. She was sick of the smell of garlic and onions and seeing her mother marinate batches of vegetables day after day, year after year. Chul was sick of it. She could use the money. Mrs. Kim was right. Neither she nor her mother doubted Chul. He would enter a college, the one that Minkyu could not attend despite all of their money. Would his mother really come and make a scene? Chul was touchy and fragile as it was. Her love was doomed. It had been. Mrs. Kim was right. Miran shook her head in disbelief; her mouth repeatedly formed indistinguishable sounds; and her feet moved along the cold, chilly hills of Sungbook. She could not have caused all this filth, Miran kept repeating in her mind. It could not have been her. If she were smarter, could she, would she have behaved differently? Could she have found a little haven for herself?

Miran's mother was not surprised when her daughter started to drive Minkyu away. Mrs. Paek had suspected his family would be difficult. She did not, however, discourage Miran, because she had seen people who could put material things aside. Why, just last year, the Hongs, who rented a room in a house two hills below, welcomed a rich son-in-law. Miran was as pretty, as generous, as talented as any girl. She deserved much more than she could give her.

Mrs. Paek also consoled herself with the thought that at least it was Miran who called it off. It was better to face the inevitable sooner than later. Miran would in time find the happiness she deserved. Despite all the songs and stories about first love, life did not end with it.

The next spring, Chul would enter the best college and be the envy of all. The possibility that he could fail did not cross Mrs. Paek's mind, as it did not cross Miran's. His success would be theirs. The tuition for the first semester would be the hardest. Afterwards, he would be able to tutor students whose parents would pay enormous amounts for students like Chul. Her son would not fail her; she would not fail him. She would find the tuition. Miran would help her, Mrs. Paek allowed herself to vaguely imagine, should she fail to save enough by the time Chul went to college.

Minkyu Kim decided to visit Miran's house before he left for America. He finished his military duty in February, but did not re-enroll at his university. Instead he would seek a new life in the States. The last time he visited Miran's house was three winters ago. A lot had changed since then. The stream disappeared, and the dirt road that meandered around the slanting houses was paved, or more precisely, covered with cracked concrete.

The turns and the windings were familiar, but he did not remember the house being so high up from the foothills. A third of way up, a wired fence blocked off the sandy cliff that had been becoming a garbage dump the last time he was here. Climb another third, he would pass Poet Han's old house, and then he would turn left and climb a few more hills before he would arrive at her house.

Miran would not be there. She was too beautiful, too talented. She never belonged here. She would have found her way out of this village, which regardless had a special place in his heart. He stopped before continuing the last few steps, before the full view of her house. Was it right for him to visit it now? What was he expecting? What would Mrs. Paek say to him? He just wanted to see and visit - before he left Korea.

He pressed toward the house. The mulberry tree behind the house, underneath it had been a chicken coop. He had not written a letter, because he too was relieved, amidst feelings of anger and disappointment, to be free of her. When asked for a reason, she said that she met a new man, which he did not believe. Yet he was glad that she told him the lies rather than the real reasons. He was not ready then - to declare his independence, get away from his parents, and be encumbered with unexamined obligations.

Passing under a clothesline, he stopped before a kitchen door and knocked it softly. No one answered. Perhaps it was better this way. He would look about the house and then leave. He was walking toward the back, when an old woman opened the door.

"Who are you looking for?"

"I came to see Mrs. Paek, who used to live here. Is she here?"

"Miran's mother? The woman who pickled?

"Yes. Is she here?"

"Aiee, gone, they left. They are rich now. They live south of the Han River. In a fancy apartment I hear. They own this house, and I am only renting it."

"Do you know how I might reach them?"

The woman sized him up, screwing her cloudy eyes. She then told him to wait and went inside.

"Here, this is their number." The old woman handed him a piece of paper.

Mrs. Paek was by the window when Minkyu came into the coffee house. She looked the same. A compact little figure, a small face with heavy waves engraved in her forehead and tight lips pulling in scores of tiny wrinkles. He bowed politely and sat across from her. The silence hung heavy.

"Why don't you call the waitress?" said she finally. "I already had mine. I couldn't sit still without one. I drank it already," ruefully smiling, she pointed to the empty cup in front of her.

"Did you wait a long time?"

"No, not at all," she said. "Uhm, I could not sleep after you called. Old age, I suppose, and nervous. I hoped you would not run into Miran."

"How is she? Is she all right?"

Mrs. Paek said that it was all her fault. She should not have let her receive so much help from him, or let him visit them so often. It was all so difficult then, and she did not see straight, she said. She also said Miran was now married to a French businessman.

"When did she meet him?"

"After you left for the military."

"How?"

"He was one of her customers, I believe," Mrs. Paek said. Did Miran then tell him the truth when she said she met someone new? Did she already know this man? Minkyu tried to recall her face as she told it to him. He shook his head. It did not matter.

"How is Chul?" Minkyu asked. How did he stomach his sister marrying a foreigner? How did that narrow, squeamish boy handle that?

"He died," Mrs. Paek said after a long pause. "The police caught him during a demonstration. He died at the police station two years ago," she added after another pause. Words failed Minkyu. Horrified, he sat silent. How did the woman before him endure it?

Mrs. Paek then pleaded with Minkyu not to disturb Miran. He promised, nodding. He had no right. Truly. He had deserted her. She had found a path. What did he expect?

He walked Miran's mother to her bus stop. After seeing her off, Minkyu walked to a nearby park on the southern bank of the Han River. It was teeming with people, despite it being a windy day and the warmth of the new spring was still faint. They came to see the low grey water, because, like him, they had no better place to go. Happier than he they may be, but they had no better place than this bit of green space amid endless rows of highrises.

The river was low. People said rain and snow did not fall as they used to. Still, the river was. Muddied and exhausted, it flowed. Slowing down at the edges and carrying on down stalling eddies, it flowed. It was not the same water in which he and Miran had rowed, full of joy on their first outing on a boat one fine day four years ago, but the river was.

Yes, yes, he would say yes. He would meet the girls his mother lined up for him. He would meet and choose. It was not a matter of love. His marriage would be stable, yes stable, like his parents'. And in time they would grow affectionate, yes, likely. He would use his mother's, no his father's yardstick and marry the best they found for him. He was part of this Han River. Miran too, part of this slow murky flow.

Sungshik

His mother called out to him as he took a few steps from Grand National Bank. It was a payday, and although he had half expected her, the sight of his mother pacing in the cold in a faded quilt coat and the heavy boots that had been his father's, flustered and rankled him, especially since his superiors and colleagues might spot her.

"Mother, what are you doing here? Aren't you cold?" said Sungshik, bowing his head briefly and leading her to a cove less exposed to the chill.

"I wanted to catch you. The wind just started. It's mild considering it is November."

"Why didn't you call? I could have come home."

"Well, it's easier this way, you being busy and all," said she, searching his face.

"Let's warm up a little. Some hot soup will do you good," said Sungshik, having thought of a nearby bistro where he could take her.

"No, no. I need to get back."

"I know mother, I know. Let's just warm you up first."

"Really, I need to get back."

"Alright, I know. Here," Sungshik retrieved a few bills from his wallet handed them to his mother.

"Now will you go with me?" he added.

"Today was your payday, wasn't it?" his mother said, while placing the bills into an inner pocket.

"Today is Saturday. As I told you before, I sometimes get paid on Monday when it falls on a weekend. It's not that much anyway."

"I suppose, when you have to pay for lodging and lunch and all," she sighed, repeating once again her misgivings about him renting a room near the bank.

"Now, let's go. Some soup, O.K.?" said Sungshik letting her remarks fall aside and refraining a retort that he usually packed his own lunch.

"No, no. I really have to get back," his mother waved away his suggestion. She started trotting and picked up her pace. He knew better than trying to divert her when she was this focused: she had a new goal, making efficient bus transfers.

"We received a letter from Aunt Miyoung," she said as they neared a bus stop.

"How is she?"

"She did not say much. She mustn't be doing well. If she had been, she would have said more. In such a far away country," she added, after ascertaining her bus was not one of those arriving at the station.

"She needs some time. She must have a lot to do," said Sungshik, attempting to lighten up his mother. He soon fell silent. She was far from him, he could see. When her bus came, she hurriedly said goodbye. Feelings of recurring guilt rose up in him. He shouted to her that he would come home the next weekend. He watched with feelings of regret and wretchedness a shabby figure looking for a seat inside the bus. She lacked the agility to claim one of the seats that were becoming empty.

Sungshik Hyun stood immobile, impervious to the chill, until senses of vexations mingled with uncertain longing returned. His mother had a way of unnerving him. She would not waste money on a bistro. She disapproved of him. He again blurted out a promise, seeking her approval. He could have done worse, Sungshik told himself.

131

Amid the weekend crowd pouring out from the buildings, shops, and buses, each armed with a thinly or thickly padded wallet, Sungshik caught a glimpse of himself in a gilded mirror of a watch store. He looked decent, more than decent in his suit and tie. A nice winter jacket would have increased the stature of his look. He meant to buy one shortly, one that would give him due weight. Buoyed on such thoughts, Sungshik stepped briskly towards the place where he would meet his girlfriend Misook.

Given his job at a bank, a teller, and his look, in addition to his new associations and stature at their church, he had great prospects with Misook. She was not half bad herself. Landing at a law office was a feat better than his. The old attorney for whom she worked was not without standing and thought highly of her. And she was charming the way she understood him without his having to spell things out. Her plain shortcoming was the crooked teeth on the left side of her mouth, which made her look toothy depending on the angle from which she was viewed. If she was seen only from the right side, she could be said to be even beautiful.

Sungshik continued on toward her office after waiting a few minutes at their meeting place, a bus stop near her office. He hoped that she would not be too late and if need be, come with take-home work, for he began to feel hungry for the Chinese meal he had in mind. The old attorney had a way of wringing more work from Misook than he should.

It was less than two years ago that Sungshik had walked through the inspection lines of the teachers and student officers on duty at the gate of his old high school. They checked that his hair was cropped closely, that his school uniform was clean, and that he wore a ribbon on his left chest, on which was written "Yushin Hunbub," the name of President Park's new constitution. No teachers or student inspectors flagged him for a violation, for his mother even ironed the ribbon and had it encased in a plastic cover so that it would not curl or unravel. Sungshik was also a good student, usually placing in the upper ten percent of his class. The bane of his life at the time was his tuition that had been accumulating throughout the school year and could block his graduation. His aunt Miyoung's visit cleared it.

Beneath the solemn gaze of President Park's portrait, which was hung on the center wall above the chalkboard, Sungshik was fiddling with a letter to a soldier on the front line, an annual school assignment he and other students performed since they could write sentences. They were told, but for the soldiers' great sacrifices on the cold frontiers and their vigilant watch that curtailed bloodthirsty North Korea, they would not have the comfort and security they enjoyed and their beloved country would be in ruins again. The least they could do was to write them thank-you letters, they were told. As he got older, however, doubts had been growing in Sungshik: he no longer passionately believed in the greatness of Korea or put stock in the teachers' promise that he would receive a reply if his letters were good. Nonetheless, he dutifully wrote greetings and his gratefulness to an unnamed soldier and as usual, was stumped on how to end it. The soldiers knew the letters were part of school assignments, and it should not matter how he ended it. But the abruptness of the ending after having said the worn phrases chafed his sense of composition even if he did not feel really responsible for it. He was writing it to receive a check mark next his name from his ethics teacher Mr. Bae, who in turn was to report a one hundred percent participation rate in this activity.

The letter writing was not so different from the public works that surfaced with breakneck urgency, whether it was to pave foul creeks overnight, or trucks spraying pesticides along the one lane dirt road to exterminate caterpillars infesting the mountains far above it, or painting slate roofs along the route of President Park's motorcade to imitate the look of tiled roofs. You did what the higher ups required on the double, without any noise about principles and justice, although there were always a finicky few, congenitally diseased, who would not let things be and would go on raising objections until the end of time. But even they must know, fine feelings of righteousness and attendant fame, or infamy, neither stilled the growling bellies nor were much of distinction when they were viewed from the timelines of the Everlasting. Sungshik was thus drifting in his thoughts, while Mr. Bae, solicitous of his own time, was not in a hurry to restart the class.

Kilsoo, his desk mate, jabbed him below the desk.

"Sungshik!" Mr. Bae was calling on him.

"Yes!" Sungshik responded smartly and straightened his posture. The principal's secretary Miss Koo stood before the class, apparently having asked for him. Sungshik followed her out. She snapped her body side to side as she moved rapidly forward in a disciplined manner. Her high-heels clicked on the wooden floor and repeatedly refreshed the echoes in the hallway. Sungshik minded that he did not fall too far behind while surmising with a disagreeable sensation that the time intervals between the calls from the principal's office must be becoming shorter as the graduation date approached.

Sungshik entered the teachers' office, where rows of desks were arranged under the ubiquitous portrait of President Park. The secretary went off to her corner next to the inner principal's office. However unpleasant were his interviews with him, Sungshik hated most the teachers who noted him with complete indifference, especially when Teacher Moon, the only one who gave off human warmth, was not in the office. The way they looked right through him made him feel worthless than dirt and led him to fantasize about his future. He would become wildly successful. They would then fawn on him and he could brush them off if he felt like it or be generous and show his superiority. Meanwhile, he told himself that their existence too was a trifle beneath President Park's solemn gaze.

Sungshik knocked on the principal's door. To his surprise, Principal Kwon opened the door immediately and invited him cheerfully into his office. He projected the quiet, learned image of gentle educator, who also required that he be treated with respect and honor. His aunt Miyoung's presence partially explained to Sungshik the principal's promptness, while generating new questions in his mind.

"You have a remarkable aunt," said the principal, as his aunt warmly greeted Sungshik with her eyes.

"I have told her she should see you before she goes. I also told her how well you are conducting yourself, in addition to being a good student. What matters is not how you begin your life, but what you make of your life. As you well know, going to college is not the end of it all. You would do well if you continued to apply yourself judiciously. I am sure you will do that. You may accompany her to the gate," he said, while Sungshik only nodded with acute attention. Pleased, he ushered them out gentleman-like, and his aunt gave him many thanks and bowed to him most respectfully.

Aunt Miyoung stepped cautiously in silence and only when they passed the last classroom and came before the double doors that led to outside, she stopped.

"How is the family?" she asked, searching his face.

"About the same," he shrugged, for Sungshik could not articulate in any other way the numbness he felt when he thought

135

of his family. The way they eked out a living could be said to be miraculous; he was not thankful. His aunt resumed after a silence.

"I wanted to see you before I left for America, which will be the day after tomorrow. This is my in-law's address in Texas." She handed him a note.

"Just in case, although I will write as soon as we get settled and have our own address in Oklahoma. They will know how to reach me, just in case."

Sungshik deciphered the handwritten English with difficulty. It was different from the kind to which he was accustomed. He placed it in his left chest pocket.

"I paid all your back-tuition. You are cleared to graduate. The principal was gracious and spoke highly of you. Please be good to your mother and tell her that I will write soon."

She then took out an envelope from her handbag and placed it in his hand. He stood gazing at it, not knowing what to do.

"It is not much. Put it away," she said. "Put it away, it's not much," she repeated.

Sungshik folded it in half and stuffed it in his pants pocket.

"Remember, you are the oldest. I don't have to say it, I know. I can't help myself. Everyone is counting on you. You will do well, I am sure. Be good to your mother and be healthy."

"You too, be careful," Sungshik said, following her out.

"In, in! Don't come out, in! Study hard!" she said, waving her hands to him and hurrying towards the grey steel gates of the school's front entrance. Breaking away from her family, tradition, and country, she still reminded him of his duties as the eldest son.

Sungshik had planned to fulfill his spur of the moment promise to his mother at the bus station on the following Sunday after the morning service at the Forever Grace Presbyterian Church. But he was walking up the familiar path toward his home with a sack of tangerines on Saturday afternoon after his shift. His mother would have been expecting him since Friday, and it was better for him to get it over with, he decided. Little Sungil, the first to see him, ran up to him and loudly announced his visit. Inside the sliding double doors, in the living space between his parents' room and the room he had shared with his younger brothers, Sungwoon was engrossed in a comic book amid piles of them. Sungkoo, the brother just below him, was at work. After his middle school, he said that he would rather go to work than continue with school; neither his parents nor his elder brother attempted to dissuade him.

Coming out of the main room, his mother welcomed him and asked him if he was hungry. Sungshik repeatedly assured her that he was not; she keenly observed him.

"I will get some hot tea ready. Do go and greet your father." His mother gathered herself and turned to go out to the kitchen.

Sungshik quietly slid open the door to the main room. His father lay supine on a thick blanket, with his eyes closed. He became continuously weaker even before he began to cough out blood, although there had been times, when the weather was mild, he seemed to improve. Shriveled, he lingered on, while his wife persevered to improve his health and conjured up strange ideas. The worst was the winter when she conceived that what he needed was fresh liver and cajoled and coerced her two eldest sons to hunt house rats and harvest their livers. Sungshik had joined Sungkoo in the hunt, because he feared the shame that would follow had he disobeyed. The fear had overruled his rationality, which said the task was not only gruesome, but also most likely without any benefit. After the hunt, he hid in his room, spreading his notes and books and pretending to study Sungkoo harvested the tiny, blood-dripping livers and strung them beneath the eaves.

Sungshik sat close to his father and watched him. His father parted his eyelids slightly and then closed them. After a while, he opened his eyes and motioned for a glass of water. It was next to his cot. While Sungshik held it, his father raised himself, leaning on his left arm. He took two sips and then motioned toward Sungshik to help him lie down. Sungshik sat on, watching his father. Dullness began to oppress him.

When Sungshik came back out to the living space, his mother had tea and steamed potatoes ready for him. She invited him to sit close to the small lacquer table.

"He does not sleep long. He will be better a little later, soon," said she and poured a cup of hot corn tea for Sungshik.

"He saw me. He looks very tired."

"He is worse today than he has been. He did not sleep well. I am sure he will be happy to talk to you a little later. He misses the company. The other day Mr. Ahn came over. Your father wore himself out, talking nonstop about the time when he canvassed for President Park," his mother said.

"That was a good time," she added.

Sungshik silently sipped his tea, indicating to his mother he was busy, and recalled the time when his father was the center of the village. He then brought home pots, pans, and other kitchenware after canvassing for President Park's Party. His mother was in charge of disbursing them to women in the village. And Sungshik was proud of his father, about whom other men of the village gathered. He amused them with anecdotes and riddles: why did a candidate who gave out rubber shoes win over his opponent, who gave out canvass shoes in his turn? His listeners sat nonplussed: a three year old would know which were more expensive. Regaling, his father revealed the secret: the district had not a bit of asphalt; the voters preferred *gomushin*, of course! When their roads turned to mud and toads, they could just rinse and wear them again. Both candidates were from Seoul and had no idea about their district; but the right candidate was elected after all! The men around him slapped their knees and agreed with him at the absurdity of it all. The father who had made his heart swell with pride on such occasions was struggling to breathe on the other side of the sliding doors, which were shielded with see-through rice paper.

"He was doing better only a few days ago," his mother broke their silence.

"Is he able to eat?"

"He had a good helping of porridge last night. Of course, he could use something more substantial."

Nodding, Sungshik sat silent. He understood the ache in it all and could not change any of it, and the silence he maintained so as not to disrupt their fragile truce rendered his visits most difficult. Several times he resisted the impulse to ask how Sungkoo was doing. He worked at a garment district in Chunggyechun, a market famous for not only its diverse merchandise and sweatshops, but also for the criminals it drew in. It was a natural swamp for such fellows. But asking about his younger brother would only highlight his failures and his family's unmet expectations. He did not ask to be the eldest son or to be born, thought Sungshik; and Sungkoo was pluckier than he and would not have succeeded in school anyway, Sungshik told himself.

"Sungshik, I know it has not been easy for you. You have your reasons for renting a room, and it hurts me to burden you. Try to understand, could you move back home? Just until the little ones are little older?" his mother said in between pauses and sighs, breaking the silence again.

"With your father like this, having you in the house would be a great help to me, and to Sungkoo, I am sure. He does not complain, you know him. It's just that, it does not seem right that he acts the man in the house. It is not right, when you are more mature and older. The little ones too, they really look up to you," she added.

"Yes, mother, I'll think about it," said Sungshik. He silenced the screams in his heart.

After another long pause, his mother resumed. "Your aunt wrote that she saw you before she left Korea, that your principal talked highly of you."

"How was she? I don't seem to remember you saying anything about it," she added, as Sungshik sat silently, without a response.

"She looked fine. She paid up my tuition. I told you, remember? What else did she say?" asked Sungshik.

"Not much." His mother became silent. Sungshik got up, indicating to her that he was going to the outhouse. Outside, he beat back the shamefulness that heated his innards. He reminded himself that the money his aunt gave him during her visit at the school would have been less than a thimbleful of snow in hell, had he given it to his mother.

As he walked home on the day his aunt visited his school, Sungshik saw, as he never had before the cafés, bistros, and shops that lined the streets and alleys near his school. He had excised their existence from his senses, but on that day it was as if they knew of the envelope in his pocket. Each time he stepped forward, repulsing the immediate lure before his eyes, he was pressed onwards to another. It was exhausting, and the stores were becoming more tempting as he made his way. Finally yielding to the temptations, he thought it fortunate that he was with his desk mate Kilsoo. He was not only gentle, but also could not refuse his offer of a plateful of dumplings: he always offered to share his lunchbox with Sungshik when he was without one, and more times than he could remember, he had spoonfuls of Kilsoo's lunch, the barley depot of their class when random lunchbox inspections were announced. Kilsoo sat with the patience of Confucius, or Jesus, while the classmates who had only white rice in their lunchboxes took his barley grains and planted them seemingly randomly in their rice.

A consequence Sungshik had not foreseen when he paid for the two platefuls of dumplings was that, soon after departing from Kilsoo, his intention to hand the rest of the money to his mother began to waver. Could his mother be able to notice his theft? He could not possibly face her and say that he did not have the will to resist the bistro. She might not even believe that was all. How could he endure his shame? She did not know about the money. She did not have to know about it. It was not much. It would not make much difference to his family. He would keep it and spend it for the family. When he reached home, Sungshik hid the money in a hole behind his dresser.

He was pleased with this foresight when he landed his job at the bank on his principal's recommendation. He used the money to buy his clothes for the job. By then he was attending Kilsoo's church and told his mother that a wealthy congregant helped him out.

"I need to get going before it gets late," said Sungshik, when he returned to the living room. His mother motioned him to sit and refilled his teacup. Whether he was deluding himself, or

141

whether he in fact used the money for the family, it was best to leave the house as soon as he could.

"Already? Wouldn't you want to see Sungkoo? Wait for him and have dinner with us," said his mother.

"I have to go, mother. I have a lot to do. There is an evening school I could attend. I need to start preparing."

"When will it start?" she asked, after a silence.

"I don't really know. Maybe this coming spring, if all goes well," he said, as the realization dawned on him that he might have erred in mentioning the school.

In between pauses, he mother said, "I know you would like to study more. You are ambitious. I am proud of you; I should be. And I know we should not stand in your way, but I think of Sungkoo too. How is your studying going to help him? Did you see your father? How long do you think your father will live?"

"I know mother," said Sungshik. His father, who had created illusions so great that he looked up to him as a giant, lay barely breathing and coughing out blood. His mother, who was fiercely protective of her family, was right to ask him these questions. Her blind passion and sacrifice for the family made her monumental to him. Had she been in his shoes, she would have done the right thing. He was not like her. He did not want to, and could not lay down his life, not now. He was to overcome his odds and shine brilliantly. He was the oldest. He owed. He would pay. A little later. After he lived; after he began to live and satisfied some of his desires. He could not give up on the tantalizing brilliance, which he saw only from a distance.

"Mother, believe me, I understand. I will consider it," said Sungshik after a pause. "I'd better get going," he added gently, getting up.

"Here, take this with you," his mother said. Sungshik sat back down, watching her take out a white tissue paper from the inner pocket of her skirt.

"Sunja brought it for me the last time she came to visit home," his mother said, unwrapping a gold band.

"Many times I thought about pawning it. This way it will stay in the family." She handed it to Sungshik.

"You keep it; it is yours!" he shouted in horror.

"Listen to me, your mother. You take it with you. I rather receive the money from you and have it within our family."

She was unmovable when she turned resolute. Even his father had learned to dress her decisions as his own when she became so. At times, he even dropped the pretension.

"Yes," Sungshik said and received it. He rewrapped the band and placed it in his pocket. He got up and bowed to his mother, who indicated that he could depart. Outside, Sungil and Sungwoon were spinning their tops, oblivious to the chill that had increased under the fading sun. He watched them with a glad heart as they saved falling tops with masterful lashes. He then trotted off, encouraging them to continue with the game and not stop it on his account. But the boys switched their attention to their oldest brother and loudly announced goodbye, bowing. The tops fell.

Sungshik fled down the hills. His mother laid a new claim on him, this time with a gold band. She hoped for a handsome accounting, he was sure. Perhaps she also reckoned it would be returned to her. She meant to accuse, for his defiance of her wishes, reminding him that it was not only Sungkoo he was betraying, but also his younger sisters. He could recount, he had thought, all of his mother's complaints and nagging; he, however, could not remember her expressing a desire for a gold

143

band, something his younger sister had gleaned. It was a good sign that Sunja could buy a ring. It meant she was doing well, Sungshik told himself.

A bus was not idling at the terminal below the hills. Flustered, he could not stand still and wait for a bus. Sungshik continued his brisk steps, momentarily reaching the place where there had been two bridges: one of them connected the road to the southern parts of the mountains, and the other led to the northern parts and to his village. The bridges were gone, but their traces remained in the ugly jutting angles of the buildings to the straightened and widened road. Their oblique angles reflected those that had been between the bridges and the road. Their traces also remained in the dilapidated signs of the old stores: Twin Bridges Butcher Shop, Twin Bridges Barbershop, Twin Bridges Real Estate, and Twin Bridges Market.

A little further down, he arrived at a major fork. One road, serviced by the buses, followed the stream that had become a subterranean sewer. The other, a short cut to downtown, was devoid of bus services until one neared the wealthier district after a long hump on the road, evidence of the hills that were razed. Sungshik, still unable to pause, pressed on over the slope, passing his old school and other handsome landmarks without noting them, until a pawnshop beneath the massive walls of the palace mushroomed to existence in his mind. He had accompanied his father to it, at first with pride and excitement, and then with mute embarrassment and resentment.

The specter of crossing the alley where the pawnshop was tucked away frightened Sungshik. He was not to act rashly while his inside churned from his memories of it, or in reaction to his conflicting feelings towards his mother's new claim. The solution he hit upon was to dash across the alley when he neared it.

He hoped it would diminish whatever pull the pawnshop might have on him.

"Hey, watch where you are going! Hello," said a familiar voice, and to his consternation, Sungshik stopped right in the middle of the lane that led to the pawnshop.

"Hey, what's wrong?" said a familiar face.

"Nothing."

"Nothing, I am sorry," Sungshik repeated.

Chul, a wonder boy of his village, a year older than he, stood watching him with amused curiosity.

"I heard that you work at a bank now. You do look your part, other than your unruly battery of your fellow pedestrians," Chul said with a grin that irritated Sungshik.

"Come, come with me," said Chul, shifting his demeanor and becoming friendly. Sungshik recovered his composure.

"It was a beautiful watch, but too shiny and heavy for me. The pawnbroker approved it and gave me more than I expected. I didn't deserve such a thing, a gift from my sister's boyfriend, you know. Come! It must be your fate to help me spend it today. Come!" Chul locked Sungshik's arm and led him. Sungshik could easily imagine, having known Chul and his family, the nature of his disclosure, even though they had grown apart since their childhood, both having learned to cope with various embarrassments and resentments with distance and reclusiveness.

"Here, here we are." Chul opened a door and expertly maneuvered them to a snug corner in the pub. It exuded western influences, from music to the posters on the walls, from the waiters' long hair to the menu with unfamiliar dishes, and from the mahogany bar to the booths and wooden tables inscribed with alphabets, indicating the transliterated initials of some lovers. The pub, whose clients were mostly college students, was

145

the kind from which Sungshik stayed away, mostly because he feared the unfamiliar.

"Here!" Chul raised his mug as the waiter set their drafts on the table. Sungshik followed him.

"Do you come here often?" asked Sungshik, noticing the waiter had an unusually lengthy and slender waist.

"I used to. You know how it is; you let go of yourself after high school. I haven't come here for a while. Even freedom gets old after a while. Besides, it's not often that I have the money, time, or inclination. And a boon companion."

Sungshik gauged silently that Chul had become much more talkative. It must be the badge of confidence that the best schools bestow on their students.

"You are very quiet. What's up?" asked Chul.

"Nothing. I don't have much to say."

"I will drink to that. I know exactly what you mean," said Chul, while getting the waiter's attention.

Two more mugs of golden liquid with slight foam presently appeared on their table. The waiter with a lengthy waist then took an order for two plates of hamburger, for Sungshik shrugged to Chul's question of what he would like and Chul doubled his choice. Although Sungshik had not been thinking of food, the prospect of it made him feel hungry. He tried to dampen the eagerness with which he anticipated the burger.

"How is the university? Is it fun?"

"At first, of course. It was bracing to be able to grow hair, wear jeans and whatever else, and especially to be able to get up after nine, if I wanted. And I thought I would really learn great things. It took me less than a semester to realize that it was more of the same, stuffing my head with formulas. I could not do it. I did not wish to go on pretending that the professors were teach-

146

ing me something and that I was learning something. I did not have it in me to figure things out on my own either."

Chul paused while the waiter placed their food on the table.

"It was a fantasy, a beautiful fantasy to study physics in Korea. I then began to frequent underground meetings. They were exhilarating, people voicing the same things I have felt for a long time and calling for action. Compared to the formulas I was to stuff in my brain and memorize, the changes they were advocating were refreshing. They are fundamental, even for our educational system."

Chul had not changed as much as he first seemed, thought Sungshik. The discontent that led him to clash with his family and those around him seemed to have channeled him to activism.

"In fact, I am going to a meeting not far from here. Do you want to come? Why not join me?"

"I don't think so."

"Just take a look. No one is going to do any harm to you. It would be an interesting experience," said Chul. "You are interested in college life, I know. In today's Korea, other than the usual dating games and school festivals that mean to keep us occupied, college life means the underground. Here is the opportunity, and you refuse. Why?" Chul said.

Sungshik maintained his silence.

"I know what you are saying. You do not have the time, the energy, or the inclination, right? I understand, of course, I do." Saying so, Chul was emptying his mug, and Sungshik felt a perverse satisfaction arising within him as he watched Chul betray his condescension despite his friendly intention. Sungshik rebuked himself for his meanness and responded to Chul.

"To tell you the truth, making a living is hard enough for me. I never seriously thought about such meetings and activism. I hear about them; they are not my affair. I cannot afford them. I am surprised you are like this. I really didn't expect you to be dragged into it. I mean, you are smart and know as much, more than I do about our reality. I can understand though, the desire for activism."

"I know what you are saying. I had thought just like you. There is truth to the perception that activism and demonstrations are for those with their bellies full. Yes, my belly is full, or I am a fool in need of a dream. It is not grand patriotism or sheer desperation that moves me, but a beautiful idea of a just society, society in which we would take our chance to be born, not knowing in whose bosom we would tumble forth, isn't it beautiful? I heard it in a lecture. The truth of it gripped me," said Chul, with quiet resolution, while Sungshik repressed the envy arising in him as he imagined Chul in a lecture hall with the leisure to imagine a utopia.

"As I said, I was a physics major. You could not fathom the blow I felt in my gut when I found doddering professors at Korea's best university. They were no different than petty bureaucrats abusing their small power. You know what I am talking about. Any Korean who has learned to walk knows it. The movement is not without its flaws; at least it gives me hope the future will be different. I feel strong and hopeful when I am with them. There really are people who risk their lives for justice, to make this country equitable."

As Chul expressed his views, Sungshik slowly digested, with awakening feelings of humiliation, the gap he perceived between them. However much Chul was disappointed in his university, it had given him the confidence, the authority to state opinions in spheres beyond his immediate concern; while he was mute in the background, toiling with all he had, to account for every penny that passed through his fingers.

"Don't worry. No one can force you to come. I was glad to see you and thought you might enjoy hearing some of today's leading dissidents. Here, let us finish our drinks and move on." Chul changed his tone to light heartedness and raised his mug, replenished with golden liquid. Sungshik followed him.

When the two exited the pub, the lampposts and store lights spilled misty halos amid early winter's chill and evening darkness. One could have a blissful time in a snug corner, decked with food and drinks and lofty ideas, thought Sungshik. He could really get used to such a life. He expanded his chest and filled his lungs with cold air. He had a way to go.

"You know where I'm going. How about you?" asked Chul. He peered intensely at Sungshik as if he were attempting to enter his brain.

"I have an errand to run, not far from here." In fact, he was to call Misook, but she could wait, thought Sungshik.

"Well, good luck to you. See you again," said Chul.

Sungshik greeted him off and watched Chul pick up his pace toward downtown and disappear in the darkness beyond the nearest lamppost. Sungshik then turned toward the pawnshop. He could use the cash. He would keep some for himself and give the rest to his mother. He thought of the envy he felt towards Chul and his lofty ideas. He shook his head. One certainly wished for a just society. But who would not desire to experience life in a castle, tasting delicacies and the glitter of merrymaking? One had to work for them. The earth could not afford them to everyone, and demolishing such experiences in the name of justice and equality would make human life unbearably dull. You were to raise yourself out the mess.

Spoiled by his doting mother and sister, Chul did not know how good he had it. Not that it was his business. He had enough

149

problems of his own. He needed to extricate himself from his family. He needed to raise himself up. He had a long way to go before he could think about other things in life. But Chul's talk was beautiful. It was refreshing, and even uplifting to hear of them, however far fetched seeking justice and fairness was in this Korea. Chul was a fool ready to squander his hard won advantages for ideals that did not exist. The world was what it was. Endless "ifs" and "buts" were songs of the Sirens. It was not his fault he was not like his mother. Nor was it his fault that he was not like his sisters Sunja and Sunhee, or his brother Sungkoo.

As he entered the shop, the pawnbroker greeted him casually and returned to his newspaper. He knew how to give space to his customers and watch them casually over the paper. Sungshik was grateful for the owner's easy manner. He was also relieved that the shop was empty of other customers. As he neared the display case, the watches attracted his eyes. Which one had been Chul's?

"I have a really good one that recently came in, if you are interested in a watch," said the shopkeeper.

"No, thank you." Sungshik moved away from the watches.

"Take your time," said the pawnbroker, gingerly flipping the newspaper. It was pasted with stories about a rich Korean millionaire captivating Washington socialites. How does one ever rise so high, wondered Sungshik and turned his gaze towards piles of rings that evidenced widely spread misery. Poverty was not his alone. Unlike them, he had plans. His ring was not another rubbish of broken promises.

Sungshik tore himself from the pawnshop. He then dashed toward a public telephone. Misook, glad to hear from him, gently directed him toward her. In churning sorrow and hope, Sungshik stepped forward. A renewed sense of acceptance moved

him. He needed not obey others' expectations. Neither was he free to disregard the hopes and affections of his family nor to inflict further careless shame upon himself. He was to thread his future, without unduly harsh judgments and steering clear of fevers for utopia and deadening paralysis.

Korean Words, Names, Events, and Practices in the Stories

March First Movement (Samil, 3-1): A nationwide mass protest that began on March 1, 1919 against the Japanese colonization of Korea. It began with a recital of the Declaration of Independence for Korea in Pagoda Park in Seoul and lasted several months. The Japanese responded with severe reprisals and killings: their accounts report that 553 Koreans were killed and that 12,000 Koreans were arrested. Korean sources report that 7,500 Koreans were killed and that 45,000 Koreans were arrested (Cumings 155).

April 19th Revolution (Sailgu, 4-19): A nationwide protest that followed the elections held on March 15, 1960 and reached its peak on April 19, 1960, when the police and military killed hundreds and injured thousands of civilians. It ended the reign of South Korea's first president, Rhee Seungman. He was airlifted to Hawaii on April 29, 1960; his henchman Prime Minister Yi Kiboong was killed by his own son (Yi *et al.* 341, 331).

May 16th Coup D'état (Oilyook, 5-16): A coup led by Colonial Park Junghee in 1961. It overthrew the civilian government that rose after the April Nineteenth Revolution and began the reign of President Park.

Korean War (Yookeo, 6-25): The war between North and South Koreas. It started on the early morning of June 25, 1950. One source estimates that 1.5 million people were killed, while 3.6 million people were injured (Yi *et al.* 315).

Korean Independence Day (Kwangbokjul): Korea became independent on August 15, 1945, following Japan's surrender to the Allies in World War II.

Beautiful Country: The meaning of "Migook," the Korean name for the USA.

Blue House: The office and residence for the President of South Korea.

Bookak Mountains: A mountain range north of downtown Seoul.

Changkyong Palace: One of great palaces of Chosun.

Chosun (1392-1910): The Korean dynasty founded by Yi Sungkye, a general who seized royal powers, thereby ending the previous dynasty, Kyoruh (918-1392) (Park 20). Chosun ended when Japan annexed Korea on August 29, 1910 (Park 456).

Gomushin: Flat rubber shoes.

Haehwa: One of the old districts in downtown Seoul near Changkyong Palace.

Hanbok: Traditional Korean dress. For women, it includes a short top with long, loopy sleeves and a fluffy skirt long enough to cover the shoes.

Han River: One of Korea's major rivers. Flowing generally from east to west, it divides Seoul into southern and northern parts.

Han Yongwoon (1879-1944): A poet, a Buddhist monk, and one of the leaders in the March First Movement.

Hongbu: A quintessential good person in the legend of *Hongbu and Nolbu*. Hongbu and Nolbu are brothers born to a wealthy family. When Nolbu, the oldest, becomes the head of the family, he expels Hongbu and his family. Penniless, they are besieged by hunger and sickness, but Hongbu never loses his humanity and acts kindly to all, including a bird with a broken leg. It returns the next spring and gives him a seed of riches. While Hongbu is handsomely rewarded for his goodness, Nolbu loses all of his possessions because of his greed and envy.

153

Hwang Jinee: A courtesan during 16th century Chosun, who was famous for her beauty and poetry.

Itaewon: A district developed because of its proximity to the U.S. army headquarters in Seoul. It caters mostly to foreigners in South Korea.

Japanese Occupation: Japan annexed Korea on August 29, 1910, thereby formally ending its protectorate status, which began in 1905.

Jongro: One of the oldest districts in downtown Seoul. It has numerous historical landmarks.

Kayakeum: A twelve stringed musical instrument with a long wooden base.

Kim Jongpil (1926 -): A nephew of Park Junghee. He was instrumental in Park's rise to power. He secured the financial means and founded institutional bases for Park's regime, including the KCIA and the Democratic Republican Party (DRP). (Cumings 353).

Kim Sowol (1902 - 1934): A poet, known for his lyrical sensibility and use of Korean language that have been said to embody an essence of the Korean soul.

Kimchi: Pickled vegetable dish, made usually from cabbages or radishes.

Korean Central Intelligence Agency (KCIA): A Korean intelligence bureau, founded by Kim Jongpil on June 13, 1961 with help from the USA (Cumings 353).

Korean floor (Ondol): The heat from the fireplace in a kitchen attached to a room is conducted through the slabs beneath the floor of the room, thereby heating it. The part of the floor closer to the kitchen is warmer than the rest.

Korean military service: A mandatory military duty on young men; it was for three years during the 1970's.

Korean names: Usually of two syllables, the siblings of the same gender often have the same first syllable: for example, the names of Sunhee's brothers in "The Horizon", Sungshik, Sungkoo, Sungwoon, and Sungil.

Korean school calendar: Schools start and end during the first quarter of a calendar year.

Korean school years: The twelve years before university education include six years of elementary education, three years of middle school, and three years of high school.

Korean watermelons: Round and much smaller than the oblong ones found in the USA.

Myongdong: A district in downtown Seoul known for its fancy shops and restaurants.

Namsan (Southern Mountain): A mountain in Seoul, located south of the Chosun palaces.

New Village Movement (*Saemaeul Yoondong*): Five year plans initiated by President Park to modernize Korea, in particular, its poor rural villages.

Pagoda Park: One of the oldest public parks in downtown Seoul. Located where there had been an old, famous Buddhist temple, the leaders of the March First Movement met here and read the Declaration of Independence for Korea.

President Park (Park Junghee) (1917-1979): The leader of the coup d'état on May 16, 1961. Toppling the civilian government that followed the April 19th Revolution, the then colonel ran as a candidate in the election held on October 15, 1963 and became the president of South Korea. He ruled Korea until his KCIA director killed him at a dinner table on October 26, 1979 (Yi *et al.* 374; Cumings 374).

President Rhee (Rhee Seungman) (1875-1965): A U.S. educated Ph.D. and the first President of South Korea. He ruled from 1948 to 1960. Unable to usher in democracy or control rampant corruption and abuses by his political associates, he was whisked to Hawaii following the April 19th Revolution (Yi *et al.* 280).

Soju: Strong rice liquor.

Shin Sungil: A Korean actor. He was popular during the nineteen-sixties and seventies.

Simchung: The eponymous heroine in the legend of *Simchung*. She sells herself to sea merchants when they come to her village looking for a sacrificial virgin. Her price is three hundred cups of rice, the amount her blind father promised to Buddha for his sight. Moved by her goodness, the sea god sends her back to the world, wrapped in a lotus flower that blossoms in a palace pond. The king falls in love with her and marries her. Queen Simchung conducts a nationwide search for her father and finds him. He opens his eyes upon hearing the voice of his dead daughter.

Sulak Mountains: A mountain range, running north to south on the east coast of the Korean peninsula. It includes the Keumkang Mountain in North Korea and the Sulak Mountain in South Korea, both famous for their palisades and fall foliage.

Ulsan: A port city in Kyongsang Province. It began to develop as a center for heavy industry under President Park.

Yi Mija: A Korean singer. Known for her trilling voice, she was immensely popular during the nineteen-sixties and seventies.

Yi Soonshin (1545-1598): A general. He fought against the Japanese invasions that lasted from 1591 to 1598. It also drew in China's Ming Dynasty on the side of Korea and included periods of lull while the parties attempted to negotiate a truce. Following the general's successes and popularity, he was accused of treason and was imprisoned in 1597, but was later reinstated to fight the Japanese. He was killed during a battle in 1598 (Park 245-49).

Yoon Junghee: A Korean actress. She was popular during the nineteen-sixties and seventies.

Yushin Hunbub: President Park's constitution devised after the close presidential election in1971. Published in October 1972, it was voted on December 1972, with an official participation rate of 91.9% and an official approval rate of 91.5% (Yi et al. 425-246). President Park's opponent during the 1971 presidential election was Kim Daejoong, the President of South Korea during the years of 1998 to 2003.

Bibliography to Appendix

Cumings, Bruce. <u>Korea's Place in the Sun: A Modern History</u>. New York: Norton, 1997.

Park, Youngkyu. <u>History of Chosun Dynasty in One Volume</u>. Seoul: Deulnyuk, 1996.

Yi, Kwangshik, *et al*. <u>Encyclopedia of Recent Korean History: 1860 - 1990</u>. Seoul, Karam, 1990.

22317524R00086

Made in the USA
Charleston, SC
16 September 2013